Legacies of War

Legacies of War

VIOLENCE, ECOLOGIES, AND KIN

Kimberly Theidon

Duke University Press   *Durham and London*   2022

© 2022 Duke University Press
All rights reserved
Printed and bound by CPI Group (UK) Ltd, Croydon, CR0 4YY
Designed by Courtney Leigh Richardson
Typeset in Portrait by Westchester Publishing Services

Library of Congress Cataloging-in-Publication Data
Names: Theidon, Kimberly Susan, author.
Title: Legacies of war : violence, ecologies, and kin / Kimberly Theidon.
Description: Durham : Duke University Press, 2022. |
Includes bibliographical references and index.
Identifiers: LCCN 2021043837 (print)
LCCN 2021043838 (ebook)
ISBN 9781478015772 (hardcover)
ISBN 9781478018384 (paperback)
ISBN 9781478023005 (ebook)
Subjects: LCSH: Rape as a weapon of war—Colombia. | Rape as a weapon
of war—Peru. | Children of rape victims—Colombia. | Children of
rape victims—Peru. | Restorative justice—Peru. | Restorative justice—
Colombia. | Women and war. | Children and war. | BISAC: SOCIAL
SCIENCE / Anthropology / Cultural & Social | HISTORY / Latin America /
South America
Classification: LCC HV6558 .T445 2022 (print) | LCC HV6558 (ebook) |
DDC 362.88309861—dc23/eng/20220114
LC record available at https://lccn.loc.gov/2021043837
LC ebook record available at https://lccn.loc.gov/2021043838

Contents

Gratitude

I began writing this book during a sabbatical that coincided with the COVID-19 pandemic. Somehow amid the turbulence and loss, I found solace in writing. I loved writing this book, revisiting conversations, field notes, friendships, and much more. My spouse, Kathleen Stauffer, has listened to me read every line out loud, and her wit and love of language helped me rediscover the joy of writing.

A Tufts University Collaborates Grant allowed me to think further about many of the issues raised in this book. With my colleague Dyan Mazurana, we convened an author's workshop at the Fletcher School, Tufts University, to discuss "Challenging Conceptions: Children Born of Wartime Rape and Sexual Exploitation." We spent several days with researchers and practitioners from around the globe, each of whom has spent decades working with women who survived wartime rape and with their children who were the result of that violence. Together we aimed to rethink some of the assumptions that echo in the literature, policy, practice, and popular culture about these children and those around them. Those conversation were illuminating, and an edited volume is forthcoming.

I thank Elisabeth Wood and a very insightful anonymous reviewer for comments and suggestions that sharpened my thinking. Libby is a role model and mentor for many of us, and academia is a better place for her brilliant kindness. At Duke University Press, Gisela Fosada and Alejandra Mejía welcomed my manuscript with an attention to detail and great care for the content.

I appreciate Dipali Anumol and Roxani Krystalli very much. They read and provided comments on this book—and provided, as well, living proof that feminist researchers rock.

As I was adding the final touches to this book, I taught my first environmental humanities course at the Fletcher School. My remarkable students made each weekly discussion a cure for Zoom fatigue. For their lively minds, great questions, political commitment, and class finales that spanned the genres of poetry, websites, op-eds, and musical scores, I thank Raunaq Chandrashekar, Ally Friedman, Hyun Kim, Rebecca Mullaley, Kelsey Rowe, Sarah Shahabi, and Rose Wang.

And still more gratitude, desde mi corazón, to the Peruvians and Colombians who have made my research a passion project. I have felt so fortunate over the years, at times gobsmacked, that I was the lucky researcher with whom you shared your time, lives, and stories. How in the world was I so blessed? Mil y más gracías.

INTRODUCTION

In early November 2019, I stood before a packed room in a recently installed gallery space, *Fragmentos*, in Bogotá, Colombia.[1] As part of the 2016 Peace Accords between the Colombian government and the Fuerzas Armadas Revolucionarias de Colombia (FARC, Revolutionary Armed Forces of Colombia), the guerrillas had turned in some thirty-seven tons of rifles, pistols, and grenade launchers. These weapons were subsequently melted down in the Colombian military's foundry, and some of that metal made its way to the artist Doris Salcedo. With the help of women survivors of conflict-related sexual violence—each woman wielding a heavy hammer to pound the metal into thin sheets—those weapons were recast as tiles that formed the floor beneath the visitors' feet. Bogotá-based Salcedo had been opposed to leaving those tons

Doris Salcedo, *Fragmentos*, 2019

of weapons intact, concerned they might be commemorated triumphantly after having caused so much pain and death in her country: "I thought, I don't want them to be monumentalized. They don't deserve to be on a pedestal and respected as a grandiose idea that we should all look up to."[2] She chose instead to design *Fragmentos* as an "anti-monument," staunch in her conviction that "weapons and war are not something that should be celebrated."

The packed audience that afternoon included a mix of nongovernmental organization (NGO) representatives, human rights activists, lawyers working within the transitional justice courts, doctors from the Ministry of Health, journalists—and an undetermined number of rape survivors. I began my talk, "Challenging Conceptions: Children Born of Wartime Rape and Sexual Exploitation." As I scanned the audience, I noticed a woman in the second row. She was clearly of *campesina* (peasant) origin, and I was struck by her rigidly straight posture and frozen face. Was I offending her? I was not sure.

There were many questions following my talk, and toward the very end a hand rose in the second row. She asked me for the microphone, which she held in one hand so that she could unwind a wad of tissue with the other. She began sobbing and the room went silent. She had been brutally raped as an adolescent and had told no one, fearful that she would be blamed for what had happened to her. With time, her swelling abdomen gave her secret away. She explained, "I knew nothing about abortions. I didn't know what to do. I started jumping off chairs, landing on my stomach. I jumped and jumped, hoping I would kill it. It was disgusting to me."[3] Her efforts to abort failed, and she gave birth to a baby boy. She paused in an effort to stop crying, but tears continued to stream down her face. "I could barely stand to look at him. He repulsed me. I didn't want anything to do with him." With time, her mother convinced her to breastfeed the baby, which magnified her disgust. Once again, her body was lent to reproductive labor she hated, this time to feed a baby she wished had never been born. Her son is now an adult, and she was unable to have any more children as a result of the damage done by the rape. She sees him from time to time, but that gives her no comfort. "Everyone has always noticed how short-tempered he is—so aggressive, so angry. I don't know what it is. He is just like that. Everyone knows he's not normal. I don't know, but I think it must be something genetic. Something is wrong with him."

* * *

This woman's son is just one of the tens of thousands of children who have been born worldwide as a result of mass rape campaigns or wartime sexual exploitation.[4] What about these living legacies of rape and sexual violence? What do we know about these children and their life chances? How might we study the intergenerational impact of their violent conceptions? Over a decade ago, in her important edited volume, *Born of War: Protecting Children of Sexual Violence Survivors in Conflict Zones*, R. Charli Carpenter asked, "Why have children born of war by and large remained invisible on the international agenda, and how can this be changed?"[5] This invisibility was even more striking given the amount of attention that has been paid to conflict-related rape and sexual violence over the past three decades. How might we understand this disconnect?

Sex at the Security Council

In March 1994, the United Nations (UN) established a Special Rapporteur on Violence Against Women, mandated to examine the causes and consequences of gender-based violence, especially rape and sexual violence targeting women and girls. Additionally, the UN's ad hoc International Criminal Tribunals for the Former Yugoslavia and Rwanda—countries where conflict-related sexual violence in the early 1990s captured international attention on an unprecedented scale—greatly advanced efforts to codify sexual and reproductive violence. The jurisprudence resulting from these two tribunals classified systematic rape and other sex crimes as war crimes, crimes against humanity, and forms of genocide. The Rome Statute of the International Criminal Court, adopted in 1998, built on and extended those advances, providing a broader basis for prosecuting sexual crimes (including rape, sexual slavery, enforced prostitution, forced pregnancy, enforced sterilization, or any other form of sexual violence of comparable gravity) as violations of international laws on war, genocide, and crimes against humanity. No longer would sexual crimes be considered merely "moral offenses" or "injuries to honor or reputation" as they had been defined in the Geneva Conventions.

On a complementary front, a series of UN Security Council Resolutions focused on the important role women play in conflict prevention, resolution, and peace-building efforts, while simultaneously denouncing the use of rape and sexual violence against women and girls in situations of armed conflict. Collectively known as the Women, Peace and Security Agenda, these resolutions (UNSCR 1325, 1820, 1888, 1889, 1960, 2106, 2122, 2242, and 2467) demand the complete cessation of all acts of sexual violence by all parties to armed conflicts, with each successive resolution lamenting the slow progress made to date on this issue. In addition to insisting on the need to protect children from rape and sexual violence in armed conflict and postconflict situations, UN Security Council Resolution (UNSCR) 2122 specifically notes "the need for access to the full range of sexual and reproductive health services, including regarding pregnancies resulting from rape, without discrimination" (2013). There is nothing said about the outcome of those pregnancies, nor about their meaning for the mothers and their children. There is a striking irony here: concurrent with the hypervisibilization of conflict-related sexual violence was the relative silence around two potential outcomes of rape—pregnancies and babies. Some feminists have argued that sexual violence is about power and domination, not sex; one can endorse this important political insight yet still insist that we must recognize the "sex" in sexual violence. Where there is heterosexual intercourse, there are erections, penetrations, ejaculations, and potential impregnations. This is sex, albeit violent, repugnant, and degrading.

In 2019, to mark the twentieth anniversary of the Women, Peace and Security Agenda's foundational Resolution 1325, the UN Security Council proposed Resolution 2467. This resolution recognizes that "women and girls who become pregnant as a result of sexual violence in armed conflict, including those who choose to become mothers, may have different and specific needs," and advocates a "survivor-centered approach" that recognizes the needs of survivors of sexual violence for nondiscriminatory access to a full range of services. The original language included references to sexual and reproductive health, triggering vocal opposition from the United States and the "right to life" block—a group I prefer to call "forced birth extremists." When the United States threatened to veto the resolution, it was watered down and the "offending" words omitted.

I suspect that one reason children born of wartime rape were and have, to some extent, remained invisible on the international agenda is because there is no reasonable way to discuss this issue from a "survivor-centered" perspective without addressing women's right to abortion—a woman's right to refuse to lend her body to nine months of reproductive labor. The Women, Peace and Security Agenda, for all its good intentions and accomplishments, is a framework that placates those for whom a more feminist agenda would be unpalatable. "Mainstreaming gender" can be a double entendre, as the feminist critique of policy is mainstreamed into an agenda that does not threaten the status quo of powerful countries or interest groups—a move that may obscure the fact that women and their children (especially their fetuses) may be located within competing rights regimes. One cannot finesse away these competing rights. This calls for an *explicitly* feminist peacebuilding and postconflict reconstruction agenda, understood to include a full range of sexual and reproductive rights, including access to safe and affordable abortions.

Despite the capitulation to conservatives in the United States, UNSCR 2467 is an important step forward on the issue of children born of conflict-related sexual violence, specifically acknowledging this category of victims in paragraph 18 and noting their distinct needs. It also requests that the Secretary-General report to the council "within two years and no later than the end of 2021" on issues related to "the equal rights of all individuals affected by sexual violence in armed conflict, including women, girls and children born of sexual violence in armed conflict" (UNSCR 2467, 2019). This is the first time a UN resolution acknowledges children born of conflict-related sexual violence as rights holders that suffer both related *and* distinct harms from the women and girls who are impregnated following acts of sexual violence. Such acknowledgment is both timely and grounds for vociferous debates. There will be a spate of new research, and feminist ethnographers of postconflict reconstruction had best be vigilant and vocal. The impact of armed conflict is obviously gendered; its ecologies and aftermaths are equally so.

Listening to the women that afternoon triggered memories of many other conversations, some of which haunt me to this day. I felt compelled to offer something more than empathy. This book is my contribution to an interdisciplinary research agenda that can bring the insights of anthropology, feminist and queer studies, and the environmental humanities to bear on developing more compassionate policies regarding children born of wartime rape—and contribute to a gendered recognition of the human and more-than-human legacies of armed conflicts. With an eye to both the debates and the potential avenues for further exploration, I draw upon my research in Peru and Colombia. It was in the highlands of Peru that I first met children born of wartime rape and encountered women's efforts to protect themselves and their children from the initial violence as well as its potentially toxic legacies. I will explore some of those efforts and their consequences before turning to Colombia, the first country to recognize children born of wartime rape as potential recipients of reparations. Moving from the written promises of the 2011 Ley de Víctimas y Restitución de Tierras, Law 1448 (Victims and Land Restitution Law) to their implementation has been challenging on many fronts. For this particular victim category, implementation requires the delicate task of balancing a child or young adult's right to know the circumstances of their birth with the rights of mothers who may be adamantly opposed to disclosing this information to anyone. This balance means working not only with the mother-child dyad but also with the fathers, families, and communities who may accept or reject these children due to concerns about multiple forms of "inheritance": rights to land and other forms of property; claims to full membership within kinship networks; and theories about the characteristics that are passed from parent to child, at times making these children seem intrinsically, even biologically, dangerous. I examine theories of transmission and "situated biologies" to consider the impact of multiple environments and their legacies, from a woman's womb to the long reach of war and its ability to "get under the skin."[6]

Under the skin—and into the land, rivers, and mountains that are more than a mute backdrop to humanly authored devastation. It is clear that armed conflict can contribute to an environment that is toxic to human health and well-being, but to leave the argument there is to reduce more-than-human entities to mere resources that exist to satisfy human needs and desires, and to measure their destruction as unfortunate but collateral damage. I wish to move beyond this instrumentalized concern for the more-than-human to consider the interspecies entanglements that make life possible in the best and the worst of times. I will consider the multiple environments in which conception, pregnancy, and childbirth unfold, environments that may lie far beyond the control of any one woman. From toxic chemicals to land mines, from rivers tinged with blood to angry mountains, there are multiple environments and actors that play a role in reproduction *and* post-war reconstruction. To capture these assemblages, we will travel the Atrato River, one of Colombia's longest and most-polluted waterways. On this river, lifeways and waterways converge; as the Atrato winds through the Afro-Colombian and Indigenous communities of Urabá, *the river gives and is life*. In recognition of the multiple forms of violence that have convulsed the region and muddied the river's waters, in 2016 the Colombian Constitutional Court ruled that the Atrato is both a victim of the armed conflict and a river with rights. Surely it is time to consider the human and more-than-human wages of war.

Waqcha: Who Comes to Mind?

When giving talks about children born of wartime rape, I also discuss war orphans to include this vulnerable and at times overlapping group. I ask my listeners to close their eyes and conjure up the first image that comes to mind when they hear "war orphan." The image is usually that of a young child, face smudged with dirt and tears, dressed in ragged clothes, curled up on a flattened piece of discarded cardboard. In addition to the recurrent child-like figure, the image is frequently racialized as well. Conflict-related sexual violence is imagined as something that happens *over there*, to darker-skinned women being abused by darker-skinned men. The politics of representation matter, and "othering" the topic of wartime rape as well is its victims and perpetrators is too common. The emphasis on "conflict-related" sexual violence has both geographic and temporal implications: somewhere else, bracketed in times of extraordinary violence, rather than right here and now as any woman or girl walks down the street—or cowers in her home.

Years of living in Quechua-speaking communities in Ayacucho, Peru, changed *my* conjuring. It was a jolt the first time a middle-aged man stood up in a communal assembly and choked up when referring to the losses he had endured during the internal armed conflict. "Waqchaqa kachkani" (I am an orphan), he uttered through his tears. As I learned, this was not a status that faded when one turned eighteen and left one's childhood years behind. It is a category of being that marks a person on various levels, for life.

"Waqcha" means orphan, and it also means "poor." The conflation is striking. To live without one or both parents is to live with affective and material impoverishment. This term often comes to mind when contemplating children born of war and the ways in which the circumstances of their birth can ripple across their lives. When we speak about "children born of conflict-related sexual violence," we are not speaking about the age of the person per se but rather about the circumstances of their conception and birth—and how those circumstances manifest across their lifetime. The needs of that person will change as they age, but the status is one that will have legacies; these are not always tragic, but they are always there. The age of the person should not be a key factor in whether they qualify for reparations; it is the circumstances of their conception and the concentration of disadvantages and forms of exclusion many of them have faced throughout their life that require remedy. That remedy will in turn depend upon a changing set of needs as the person passes from childhood into their adult life.

I struggled with what terms to use to refer to these children, adolescents, young adults, and elderly people, all of whom could claim the status of *waqcha*, all of whom may be the result of violent conceptions. The most frequent term in the literature is "children born of war"; this is, however, policy speak. "Children born of war" lacks an agent or a perpetrator, and war itself does not impregnate anyone. The language of policy documents may not be the language that allows us to think clearly in our research. Research categories demand greater precision. An anthropologist wants details about age, gender, race, religion, nationality, culture; in short, a researcher needs to incorporate intersectionality into her questions, her categories, and her analysis.[7] The failure to incorporate other identity markers evokes "the danger of a single story." As Chimamanda Ngozi Adichie eloquently argues, "The single story creates stereotypes, and the problem with stereotypes is not that they are untrue, but that they are incomplete. They make one story become the only story."[8] I will share with you numerous stories, some of rejection and pain, others of love and care.

1

BEYOND STIGMA

I was pleased to present some preliminary thoughts on the issue of wartime rape and its legacies at a conference in London in September 2017. I had prepared my talk on the plane—not an unprecedented move on my part—and before receiving a copy of the document that framed the event and our agenda. I had not realized we would be joined by the Prime Minister's Special Representative on Preventing Sexual Violence in Conflict, with the purpose of launching the United Kingdom's *Principles for Global Action: Preventing and Addressing Stigma Associated with Conflict-Related Sexual Violence.*[1] The concept paper framing our event drew from this broader set of *Principles*: "Stigma and Children Born of War."

It was too late: my PowerPoint was ready to go. Slide 2 included a quotation from my 2015 article "Hidden in Plain Sight."

The Names . . . and Who Does the Naming?

The concept of stigma is frequently applied to these children, yet is that really all we can say about these names? Stigma seems a thin explanation for a thick phenomenon and forecloses a broader repertoire of potential meanings and motivations.

—THEIDON, "Hidden in Plain Sight," 194

It was not my most gracious moment. Nowhere to go but forward, I acknowledged the importance of the initiative, and my reservations. Word associations matter: when people hear these associations often enough, they may begin to assume there is some essential connection between the signifier and the signified. This resonates with Ian Hacking's caution that there can be a "looping effect" created by categories and classification systems; the looping refers to an iterative, self-reinforcing dynamic by which initial assumptions about salient causal relations become naturalized such that other possible alternatives are obscured.[2] The concern is that the categories can erase the tracks of their own ontology, conflating the reality of the categories with the reality of those who are sorted into and inhabit those categories. Although the UK's *Principles* seeks to diminish the stigma and discrimination these children (and their mothers) may experience, each time the phrase "Stigma and Children Born of War" rings forth, words and the world they construct are reinforced. The connection must be pried open lest stigma seem universal, even inevitable.

This policy document is not unique in its language. Indeed, in the literature that does exist, "the concept of stigma is frequently applied to these children" and given wide-ranging explanatory power. Stigma here, stigma there, seemingly stigma everywhere. Not so fast. From an anthropological perspective, "stigma seems a thin explanation for a thick phenomenon and forecloses a broader repertoire of potential meanings and motivations" for the acceptance or rejection of these children by their mothers, families, and communities.[3] Stigma appears to be a placeholder in the literature rather than an analytically nuanced tool.

I advocate specificity and explanatory pluralism, and I am influenced by Elisabeth Wood's agenda-setting work on sexual violence. In a series of influential essays, she has persuasively argued that there is tremendous variation in the use, forms, and extent of sexual violence during war.[4] Drawing upon her comparative research, Wood has employed the concept of a "repertoire of violence" to study the use, or absence, of sexual violence within and across armed conflicts. She has found that different forms of violence do not co-vary; in other words, even in highly violent conflicts, the use of sexual violence may be either very low or virtually nonexistent. This has led her to state that rape is not inevitable in war, from which follows a series of important consequences.[5] Investigating this variation moves beyond essentializing arguments about men, guns, and testosterone: understanding variation allows us to identify those factors that encourage—or may serve to limit—the deployment of sexual violence in the context of war.

Challenging the inevitable stigma narrative can lead to new and important questions. If these children or young adults are rejected by their families and their communities, what are the underlying logics that prompt this rejection? Is it the potential claim these people may have on emotional or material resources? Will they attempt to insert themselves into kinship networks that may determine the inheritance of land or the distribution of livestock? Does the gender of the child or young adult influence how others perceive them, with male children of greater concern when gender dictates inheritance? Economic motives can be addressed if we analyze them and work with families and communities to develop measures that might lessen economic fears.

In other cases, is rejection or discrimination based upon religious beliefs or practices? For some, the fact that these children were born out of wedlock is the issue, not so much that they are the product of rape. In those contexts, working with religious allies (or countering religious actors who refuse to budge on the issue) may be a key factor in assisting the children and their mothers in rebuilding their lives amid family and communal networks.

There will be other cases in which children or young adults born of wartime rape are seen as children of the enemy, reflecting patriarchal biologies and theories of transmission. In Peru I was told several times that these children would grow up and seek revenge on the people they held responsible for what had happened to their parents during the internal armed conflict; allowing these children into the family provoked fears of the familiar made strange and perhaps lethal.

And what of love and acceptance? As Wood found with sexual violence in war, absence can be evidence of a different sort. The same is true for children born of conflict-related sexual violence. For example, Dyan Mazurana found that in Mozambique, these children faced no discrimination due to their violent conception; indeed, to ask about possible stigma was to receive a puzzled look in response.[6] What possible responsibility could a child have for the way they were brought into this world? To assume that stigma is inevitable preconditions the researcher to look for it even where it may not exist. Surely one wishes to know more about the factors that allow for reintegration and affection to flourish. It may be that matrilineal societies reckon kinship in ways that challenge patriarchal notions of paternity and property. In sum, the questions proliferate when the researcher moves beyond stigma and into the realm of practical kinship and lived experience. I suspect it is in that "beyond" where promising research and answers lie.

For now, back to slide 2, and "the names . . . and who does the naming?" As we shall see, it is not only researchers who grapple with what to call "children born of war."

Entanglements: What's in a Name?

Children born of rape are a taboo.

—ELISA VAN EE AND ROLF J. KLEBER, "Growing Up under a Shadow"

Sometimes we anthropologists select our projects, but I suspect that even more frequently our projects pick us.[7] It can begin with a conversation that raises the hairs on the nape of one's neck; it can be a furtive look shared among people when asked about the history of armed conflict in their village; it may be a name that lands upon one's ear and worms its way into memory. That has certainly been the case with women, children, and rape.

I conducted years of research in the central highlands of Peru, exploring the legacies of lethal violence among "intimate enemies."[8] As with other civil wars, the 1980–2000 internal armed conflict in Peru involved high levels of intra- and intercommunal violence, which left a legacy of distrust, rancor, and landscapes steeped in blood and memories—and people painfully aware of the danger human beings can pose to one another. In addition to civilian participation in the violence, the Peruvian state installed military bases throughout the countryside; this counterinsurgency strategy led to the conflation of "terrorist-guerrilla" with "brown-skinned peasant," resulting in the destruction of hundreds of peasant communities. Within the repertoires of violence deployed by various armed groups, forms of sexual violence were one constant.[9] This violence left its own legacies: unwanted pregnancies and, at times, unwanted children. Some of these children were sent to live with extended family members residing outside the community, while others were raised by their mothers amid the gossip. I recall one communal authority who bitterly complained about *los regalos de los soldados* (the soldiers' gifts) who were born in his pueblo. That community alone had more than fifty young people who carried only their mother's last name—their father's identity was never determined.

Over the years, I met several children who were the result of rape. Here I mention just one boy whose mother had been passed around by the soldiers in the base that had overlooked their community for almost fifteen years. I first noticed him because he was standoffish, never joining the growing group of children who made my room a lively place. I tried to speak with him a few times, but he had no interest in conversation. After months of living in the community, I finally had an opportunity to ask someone about him. It was late afternoon and I saw him heading down the steep hill toward home, his three goats and one llama kept together with an occasional slap of a slender stick. The woman sitting at my side knew him by name: Chiki. My face must have expressed my surprise because she whispered that his mother was "one of those women."

Chiki is a painful name for a young boy, who in turn was a painful child for his mother. *Chiki* means "danger" in Quechua and in daily usage refers to a warning that something bad is about to happen and should be averted. People recall the ways they learned to look for a sign that the enemy might attack. One such *chiki* was a strong wind that blew through the village, rattling the aluminum roofs and letting people know something evil was about to occur.

This boy was a "future memory," a perverse distortion of time. He could not be a warning; it was too late to avert this particular danger. Rather, he was the product of an evil event his mother had been unable to escape. His mere being extends his mother's memory both to the past and into the future. Her son is a living memory of the danger she survived as well as a reminder that nothing good could possibly come from this *chiki* she had failed to avoid.[10]

I have carried Chiki's story with me for many years now, unable to write him out of my memory. He is my Child Zero, the one who set me thinking about these issues. He haunts me, and his name is clearly not an isolated phenomenon. In any given community—this is in no way limited to Peru— there is the audible impact of names, both individual and collective, that are frequently of an injurious nature. Linguistic or cultural variation alone does not explain this widespread practice in postconflict settings. Comparative ethnographic data are important because this allows us to see patterns in what at first glance might seem to be isolated cases. Time and again, across regions, names reveal the conjuncture of painful kinship and "poisonous knowledge."[11]

Some examples of these are:

Bosnia: "mixed meat"[12]

Colombia: "paraquitos" (little paramilitaries), "hijos de los verdes" (children of those in green, referring to soldier's uniforms), "hijos de Plan Colombia" (children of Plan Colombia, in reference to the increased military presence due to US funding)[13]

East Timor: "children of the enemy"[14]

Guatemala: "soldadito" (little soldier)[15]

Kosovo: "children of shame"[16]

Nicaragua: "monster babies"[17]

Peru: among other names, children are referred to as "los regalos de los soldados" (the soldier's gifts), "hijo de nadie" (nobody's child), "fulano" (what's his name), and "chatarra" (stray cat).

Rwanda: collectively labeled "unwanted children," "children of bad memories," "children of hate," "genocidal children"; and the individual names include "little killer," "child of hate," "I'm at a loss," and "the intruder"[18]

Uganda: "only God knows why this happened to me," "I am unfortunate," "things have gone bad"[19]

Vietnam: "dust of life" and "American infected babies"[20]

Although concealment is a leitmotif in the literature on children born of war and is generally understood as a way to avoid discrimination for both the mother and her child, these names are striking and challenge the assumption that rape and other forms of sexual violence are always shrouded in secrecy and silence. For instance, in their work with rape survivors in Rwanda, Elisa van Ee and Rolf Kleber found that "out of shame, many women who have been raped want to hide their trauma and the way their child was conceived."[21] This is clearly true for many women, but not for all. When it is the mothers themselves who name the child—who publicly mark their child who was born of rape—then we need to consider other psychological and social logics.

While not *all* children are given injurious names, in every context there are inevitably some names that mark these children and reveal their violent origins. As Gabriele Vom Bruck and Barbara Bodenhorn note, "Because others usually name us, the act of naming has the potential to implicate infants in relations through which they become inserted into, and ultimately will act upon, a social matrix. Individual lives thus become entangled—through the name—in the life histories of others."[22] Naming is verbal, audible, and interpersonal; naming practices are one way of expressing, perhaps projecting, the private into public space and laying claims upon others. These "entanglements" are worth contemplating. While the evidence does not allow for totalizing claims, these names surely have something to do with memory and memorialization, and with theories regarding what is passed from parent to child. Hence my insistence on *who* and *what* is being named, and why.

One of the entanglements that interests me is that of war, which is apt to include both complicity and betrayal as well as solidarity and acts of courage. In the context of intimate enemies, people have most likely seen family members, neighbors, and even themselves engaged in acts they may previously have deemed impossible. In Peru, Quechua speakers use various terms to refer to the war years: one term is *sasachakuy tiempo* (the difficult time). The *sasachakuy tiempo* is described as a time of hallucinatory realities, when the line between the real and the surreal blurred. What could be more surreal than seeing a soldier grab a chainsaw to butcher someone? How not to doubt one's own eyes when watching a guerrilla cut out an elderly woman's tongue because she dared to cry for help?

People insisted that even nature was altered, underscoring the human and more-than-human impact of war. Birds flew in foreboding formations, mountain gods took umbrage when it became too dangerous for villagers to take them offerings, and rivers ran red with blood. In one village, Tiquihua, an elderly man's eyes shone as he recounted those years: "When I remember, it makes me want to cry. What could this pueblo have done to make such things happen? I'm not lying, but the sun didn't shine normally. It shined a different color. It was like a punishment."

Among the environmental entanglements was a social matrix made volatile as distrust spread throughout families and communities.[23] As with other internal armed conflicts, the enemy could be one's brother, neighbor, or the community that lay just across the valley. Security was a key concern, and the gendered aspects of security were abundant. Under threat of guerrilla attacks, authorities in many highland communities petitioned for the installation of military bases for "protection." These communities experienced a staggering level of sexual violence. Whose security was prioritized and at what price? Communal agreements implied certain sexual agreements, negotiated for the collective good. The men in those communities built the military bases that multiplied throughout Ayacucho during the violence: women and girls "serviced" the troops. In some communities, sex became a commodity as women began selling sex. Far more common, however, was rape—and in some villages the raping was not entirely random.

In Peru, women were raped in front of their families and communities; at times they were hauled off to nearby military bases and returned with their hair shorn as a mark of the gang rapes they had endured. These violations frequently occurred with the complicity of local authorities—all male—and the neighbors who turned a deaf ear to the screaming next door, silently hoping they would not be next. I learned that officials in an untold number of military bases demanded a communal counterpart in exchange for the "security" they provided to rural communities during the internal armed conflict.[24] That counterpart consisted of food, wood, and *warmis* (women). At times this "supply" was veiled by the term *aynicha*, a diminutive of *ayni*. *Ayni* refers to reciprocal labor exchanges by which people work on one another's agricultural plots. It implies reciprocity, but with an element of hierarchy and obligation.

Ayni was placed to new ends during the internal armed conflict. Communal authorities would indicate to the military officials which houses were occupied by single mothers and widows; these homes would be targeted when the soldiers descended from the bases at night for "la carnada"—literally "bait," but in this context it refers to gorging on meat (*carne*), that is, the women they would rape. The authorities were local men, and most continue to live in these same communities.[25] Women live with the proximity of betrayal and, in some cases, their rapists.

They also live with public secrets—that which is known but not acknowledged, such that the "drama of revelation [often] amounts to the transgressive uncovering of a 'secretly familiar.'"[26] The secretly familiar in these communities was the prevalence of rape, the sacrifice of certain women in the name of the collective good, and the babies that were born as a result of *la carnada*. Chiki's mother was one of those women, gang-raped by the soldiers who occupied the base in her community for almost fifteen years. She had been marked for *aynicha*, and in turn had marked her son with his injurious name. What are we to make of this? What might motivate a rape survivor to name her child in such a way as to entangle him with her painful past, and to force others to confront that past each time they speak her child's name?

I began searching for other examples and possible explanations and came upon a fascinating piece on children born to young women who had been abducted and made "wives" by the Lord's Resistance Army in Uganda. In this article, Eunice Apio briefly discusses naming practices. In a sample of sixty-nine children, she found that forty-nine of them had injurious names (the others had been named either by the father after one of his relatives or by medical staff who delivered the babies following their mother's reintegration). Thus it can be inferred that the mothers named these forty-nine children, and the names depicted the plight of their mothers. "These names compile all the bad experiences of a mother into a name and give it a life in the nature of her baby. In this way the baby is turned into a living reminder of her suffering."[27] Of particular interest is the mother's reaction to the efforts of social workers to give these children new names such as "I am fortunate" or "Things have turned good." As Apio found in her interviews with World Vision staff, "The mothers, however, are reluctant to pick up these changes. *They prefer the old names.*"[28] We are not told why. This example, however, is at odds with the idea that women inevitably seek to conceal the violent conception of their children. When it is the mother herself who does the naming, and in doing so names the violence she survived, that intimate violence is moved outward into the public domain where it may have been known but not acknowledged. While the children themselves may serve as reminders to their mothers of the initial violation, the names serve to remind others of a painful past. This appears to be less about shame than it is about pressing some sort of claim upon others—from poisonous knowledge to a demand for acknowledgment? Why are the mothers breaking this particular silence?

Naming is both a "saying" and a "doing," and speaking these names implicates others in an act of memorialization. Might this be, at times, a woman's refusal to accept shame and stigma, albeit at a cost to the well-being of her child? In women's testimonies to the Comisión de la Verdad y Reconciliación del Perú (CVR), or Peruvian Truth and Reconciliation Commission (PTRC), they narrated the familial and communal consequences of the internal armed conflict: women were bearers of collective history. Women were also *disruptive* of communal histories that had frequently been elaborated by community leaders, virtually all of whom were men, and whose official histories turned overwhelmingly on masculine bravery in defense of their communities and "their" women.[29]

Anyone who has spent time in a rural community knows that we are far from the romanticized image of the "Andean community" as an eternal and harmonious entity. "Community" is a strategic and constructed identity, and its maintenance involves processes that seek to perpetuate communal hegemony. Although communal processes attempt to maintain "community" because villagers derive some benefit from belonging to a collective, this does not mean that all members of the collective feel the community offers equality or justice. Just as the power of speech—the authority to narrate the war years—remained in the mouths of men, so too did the administration of justice remain in their hands.

In each community there was an official history for those who came around asking about what had happened during the internal armed conflict. For example, former president Alejandro Toledo visited a community in northern Ayacucho in October 2002; this village had been the site of a high-profile massacre during the war, and his visit was timed to coincide with the work of the PTRC. That same morning in the assembly, all the men lined up in military-style formation, some with rifles slung over their shoulders. The village mayor called the assembly to order and reminded all the men that "journalists will come today. You don't have to talk with them. If they ask us anything, we're going to say we don't know the truth." The men all nodded in agreement. The mayor then glanced toward a group of widows sitting along the edge of the field. "And watch it—we don't want any of the women saying things that aren't certain." The authorities in this community, as in others, closed narrative ranks with respect to the war and their participation in the conflict. However, people who are marginal to the working of power, particularly narrative power, may have other perspectives regarding the histories of their pueblos.

Perhaps these women are "countermemory specialists" whose versions of events often diverged from the seamless accounts of the war that were offered up to those who came around asking questions. These children's names can be a form of narrating the past, of attesting to the legacies of sexual violence in the present, and of denouncing the harm that was done and for which no redress has yet been found. Amid the rhetoric of "breaking the silence" regarding rape, these women were engaged in speech acts that laid bare the brutality they endured; these names may be one component of a "vocabulary of violation" that names the profoundly gendered burden of unwanted pregnancies and children.[30] These names may be a woman's refusal to shoulder the shame for an act of violence done to her, at times with the complicity of those around her. These names express pain and in equal measure may serve to cast judgment on those who would dare to blame these women for the violence they survived.

In the literature on rape, women frequently appear as metonyms for the nation, the community—for some collective that is allegedly attacked via the rape of its female members. Indeed, the "rape as a weapon of war" approach turns on this idea and on the deployment of rape as a strategic means of achieving an end. Maria Eriksson Baaz and Maria Stern rightly challenge this framework, noting that the uses and meanings of rape are far more variable than the "weapon of war" approach allows.[31] If rape is, however, at times used to undermine the morale of the enemy and to destroy communities, then marking these children may be a way of bearing witness to the harm done to these women with the complicity of the collective.

I wish to be clear. Too often, raping women is taken to be an attack on the community via the attack on men whose honor the women's chastity is alleged to preserve. Thus women's bodies, and their pain, are reduced to a medium through which men communicate with men, women a mere canvas upon which acts are performed to "emasculate" the men in an enemy group. That is definitely not my argument. I am not arguing that we frame the raping of women as damage done to the group because it threatens male honor—far from it. I am arguing that these names indict a communal failure and the lack of solidarity with women who were the most structurally vulnerable: single women and widows, women who did not have the (symbolic?) protection of a man in the household. Public secrets involve complicity and knowledge that is not acknowledged. The names women gave their children can be interpreted as a refusal to accept the communal agreements to which they were sacrificed, and as a means of shifting the shame onto those who did nothing to stop the violation then, and who must acknowledge that failure now when they utter these children's names. Communal damage done is not, from this perspective, the damage to patriarchal notions of honor that feminists have rightly criticized: the communal damage denounced by these names is the violation of social norms and the failure to respond to the pain and suffering of another. Women's bodies have too frequently served as collateral damage in the context of war; these names thrust the harm into the faces of those who committed crimes of omission or commission, thus entangling these women and their children in an act of defiance, entangling them in the life histories of those who might have acted well but did not. In these villages, names can be one way to shame the communal elites who marked these women for abuse, and to shame those community members who remained silent and failed in their responsibility to and for others they knew—others they knew were being subjected to brutal acts of sexual violence, perhaps right next door.

The Law of the Father

The child shall be registered immediately after birth and shall have the right
from birth to a name, the right to acquire a nationality and, as far as possible,
the right to know and be cared for by his or her parents.

—United Nations Convention on the Rights of the Child, 1989, Article 7.1

I wish now to turn from first names and nicknames—and the myriad psychological and social logics at work—to the realm of surnames and governance. One's surname is "a first and crucial step towards making individual citizens officially legible, and along with the photograph it is still the first fact on documents of identity."[32] This first step in becoming legally legible to the state (and in designating the baby's nationality) is a moment in which identities are fixed and moral careers are set in motion.[33] Given a child's right to a name, let us consider "proper names" and the law of the father.[34]

In Spanish-speaking countries, such as Peru, children have two last names listed on their birth certificate and subsequent Documento Nacional de Identidad (National Identity Document). The first surname is their father's, and the second is that of their mother. For example, if one's father is Jaime Salinas Morales and one's mother is Jacinta Quispe Rimachi, the child's last name would be Salinas Quispe and recorded as such by personnel at the health post and subsequently by the municipal Civil Registrar—along with the parents' occupation, among other data. Where this becomes complicated is when the father refuses to officially recognize his child and assume his parental obligations, or when the mother does not know who the father is.

In women's testimonies to the PTRC, they indicated that Sendero Luminoso (Shining Path) commanders attempted to limit births by forcing girls and women to have contraceptive injections or abortions; in those cases in which women did become pregnant and give birth, the children were usually taken away. The military, in contrast, left many children behind. Recall the communal authority who bitterly complained about *los regalos de los soldados* (the soldiers' gifts) who were born in his pueblo and whose fathers' identities were never determined. If no father's name is given—or the father's name is unknown—the child may carry his or her mother's last two names (which is still a mark of murky conception). Importantly, these documents will register two surnames as a legal requirement of the state. While this is a form of reproductive governance, for women it is also a crucial point at which to secure the father's identity and responsibility to the child.[35]

During the internal armed conflict, members of the Peruvian armed forces engaged in widespread rape, which resulted in an unknown number of pregnancies. The PTRC registered more than seventy military bases and barracks in which acts of sexual violence were committed, which allowed the Commission to state that in certain times and places, the use of sexual violence was systematic and generalizable.[36] In my research, this assertion holds true for each community in which the military established a base during the internal armed conflict.

One component of the PTRC's work in Peru included *estudios en profundidad*—detailed case studies of certain regions or themes that allowed the Commission to establish patterns to the violence in an effort to reveal chains of command and accountability. When it completed its work, the PTRC handed certain *casos judicializables* over to the Public Ministry for further investigation and potential prosecution. One such case involved Manta and Vilca, communities located in the province of Huancavelica in the central sierra. The names of these communities have become synonymous with the armed forces' use of sexual violence during the internal armed conflict and the impunity with which they did so.

In 1983 a state of emergency was declared in the province of Huancavelica, and military counterinsurgency bases were established in Manta and Vilca, where they remained in operation until 1998. In addition to theft, arbitrary detentions, assassinations, and torture, there was the systematic use of sexual violence against women. The PTRC determined that the use of rape and other forms of sexual violence was tolerated and, in some cases, encouraged by the commanding officers stationed on site.

Just as there was a pattern to the raping, there was a pattern to the names on birth certificates. Numerous women became pregnant in Manta and Vilca, and their testimonies describe the futility of attempting to persuade commanding officers to order their subordinates to recognize and assume responsibility for the children born of rape. As one woman related, when she went to the coronel to ask for information about the soldier who had raped her, the coronel told her, "He is serving La Patria and you cannot denounce him."[37]

In the district of Manta alone, the PTRC discovered thirty-two cases of children whose fathers were military men who had refused to recognize them. The man in charge of the Civil Registry in Manta confirmed to the PTRC that the fathers of those children were soldiers who had been stationed in the district. In these cases—which frequently involved gang rape by soldiers operating under the cloak of their nom de guerre—women may not have known *who* the father was, but they did know *what* he was. In an effort to have these children recognized by their biological fathers, the mothers registered these children with either the nom de guerre or the military rank of the biological father: "Soldado," "Capitán," "Militar," "Moroco" (slang for soldier).[38] Thus names such as Edwyn Militar Chancasanampa began to appear.[39] The Civil Registrar also recorded the father's occupation: "Servicio militar."[40] The *fuerzas del Estado* (forces of the State) left a generation born of violence in their wake and, as one NGO worker noted, "it was considered something bad to have had a soldier's child, and people discriminate against these children now."[41] Armed agents of the state forcefully produced these children, and representatives of the state in turn exercised the right to impose a name should the mother fail to provide one. In the health posts and the office of the Civil Registrar, the law of the father was enforced during the baby's first interaction with the state.

Although these names did and do confer a marked identity, women still insisted on registering their children and insisted on somehow naming the father. For the women, these were efforts to secure their children's legitimacy on multiple levels. Women were calling upon the state—in the form of personnel in the health post and the Civil Registrars—to assist them in holding these soldiers responsible for what they had done and accountable to the child that resulted. There is irony at work here. Women who had been raped by soldiers serving La Patria found themselves turning to state functionaries in an effort to force the state to acknowledge the paternity of their children and to assume some form of responsibility for them. Again, what is being named and why? Women have explicitly stated to my colleague Edith Del Pino that these are "children of the state." Women found a way of putting a name to the crimes attributable to the state as it waged a counterinsurgency war on its own citizenry—or at least on that portion of the citizenry that had always been marginal to the nation. These names are both an accusation and a demand, registered on the baby's first official step toward becoming Peruvian.

Statecraft: Documents and Disclosure

A key site in which statecraft is practiced is sexuality and reproduction. "To put it bluntly, the birth of a baby is not only a matter of the family itself, but also a state affair."[42] This is true for countries at peace, and certainly for those at war. There are always policies—implicit or explicit—put in place to address the issue of children born of wartime sexual violence, the women who may abort or give birth to them, and the biological fathers. From state militaries to irregular forces, from combat troops to international peacekeeping missions, the question of what will be done with the children who (inevitably?) result from these encounters is a topic of discussion, politics, and policy making.[43] From the law of the father to the requirements of La Patria, I agree with Patricia Weitsman's assertion that "once born, the identity of war babies is inextricably linked to their rapist fathers."[44] This linkage operates in various spheres; here I wish to focus on documents.

If birth certificates are the first step in becoming legible as a citizen, these certificates set in play a series of potential points of forced disclosure. Many of us may not look at our birth certificate, tucked away in family archives, until that document is necessary for a national identity card, school enrollment, or registering for a university exam: at each of those bureaucratic junctures, the issue of disclosure becomes a central concern for many mothers, fathers, and children who may not have known the violent circumstances of their conception. For other children and young adults, disclosure may confirm what they had always suspected, having felt they were treated differently by their mothers and other family members. Whether it shakes the ground beneath them or confirms long-standing suspicions, disclosure is not an emotionally neutral event.

I know of two cases in which the question of disclosure has been systematically investigated, and both involve work and research conducted in postgenocide Rwanda. The first part of this discussion will focus on Samuel Munderere, who has worked for thirteen years with the Survivor's Fund Rwanda (SURF). His work provides an excellent example of the role NGOs can play in generating important findings; although he does not consider himself a researcher, his work directing a program that provides education and counseling services to 850 youth born of rape during the genocide—as well as working with their mothers—has given him tremendous insight into the challenges these survivors face.[45] We then turn to the cutting-edge research of Myriam Denov, who, with her Rwandan colleagues, has conducted extensive research on youth born as a result of rape during the genocide. Via interviews and focus groups with sixty young adults, her findings give us much to consider regarding the pros and cons of disclosure and how to balance a mother's right to privacy with her child's intense yearning to know more about their biological origins and heritage. Taken together, these case studies can provide recommendations to inform the Colombian Victims' Unit as it implements the first reparations program for children born of wartime sexual violence.

Samuel Munderere has worked extensively with women survivors of the Rwandan genocide, during which women were subjected to sexual violence on a massive scale, with an estimated twenty thousand children born as a result of rape.[46] Munderere is a tall, gentle, soft-spoken man who was born and raised in Uganda by his single mother, herself a Rwandan refugee. He studied to be a social worker, returning to Rwanda as an adult who was deeply moved by what he heard and saw. Munderere was surrounded by women reeling from loss and grief, and after two weeks spent working with Plan International, he returned to Uganda. Once home, he discussed his experience with his mother, who comforted him as he cried. With her encouragement, he decided to return to Rwanda and follow his passion, however much it lacerated his heart. As he tells it, "I think that I liked the job more because of the words from my mother, but also because of the experience that I had been brought up by a single mother. Having seen how she struggled to bring up my sister and me, I wanted to do something for women who were in a similar situation. So that motivated me in this job. It is not that I am stronger today—I still cry and get upset when I meet people with horrible experiences and listen to their stories—but I reflect on the conversation I had with my mother."[47]

When we spoke at a workshop on children born of wartime rape, Munderere nodded when the topic turned to birth certificates and the challenging dynamics they set into motion. In Rwanda, it is taboo to give birth outside of marriage, let alone to give birth as a result of rape. Women found themselves inventing surnames on their children's birth certificates, and those surnames have an afterlife, so to speak. As he explained:

> I think these children should be allowed registration without the name of the father. When these children reach the age of getting national ID cards, they have issues because they don't know who the father is and the mother needs to give them a fake name, like the name of an uncle. The first recommendation would be to make it easy for these children to be registered. This also applies to places like schools. Young people are asked for the names of their father and mother when appearing for the national exam. If the father is not known, they are not allowed to register. So, they have to ask their mother. This process of forced disclosure can be traumatizing for the mother. I think making it easier for the young people to register is important.[48]

Munderere is not arguing against disclosure per se but rather is opposed to forced and abrupt disclosure that occurs without emotional preparation and sustained counseling for both the mother and her child. Many of the women participating in SURF's programs had never spoken with anyone about the sexual violence they survived. Thus the first step is offering the mothers a safe space to share their stories and to realize they are not alone. In his experience, despite the initial challenges and emotional complexity of disclosure, with time the young adults with whom he works overwhelmingly expressed that learning about the circumstances of their conception and birth helped them resolve ambivalent feelings they had about their identity and sense of belonging.[49] Although the information is initially painful—and the process of disclosure requires counseling with both the mother and her child—ultimately most of the young adults felt that disclosure constitutes a form of reparation. The unsettling sense of not-knowing-but-suspecting was a hindrance to their relationships with their mothers; for a number of the mothers, in turn, having their child understand why they had been abrupt, indifferent, or distant was one step in founding a closer relationship with their children. Despite these potential benefits, however, Munderere *insists that the choice of disclosure belongs to the mothers*: it is their right to determine when and how to speak with their children—their right to decide when they have sufficiently addressed their own trauma and can then begin to think of disclosure as healing for themselves and ultimately beneficial for their children.

These findings resonate with the participatory research Myriam Denov and her Rwandan colleagues have conducted with sixty young adults born as a result of rape during the genocide. These young people are now nineteen to twenty-one years old and had much to say about their complicated lives. Overwhelmingly they had struggled with a sense of identity and belonging, the majority having been rejected by their mother's family and community. Importantly, all sixty of them stated that they fervently wished to learn about their biological fathers and yearned to know the "truth" about their origins.[50]

This desire is not surprising, but it is worth pondering. Debra DeLaet has noted that acts of sexual violence that result in conception often negate the mother's contribution to her child's identity.[51] Patriarchal biology meets patriarchal kinship systems and inheritance to the detriment of both the women and the children they forcibly bear. Inheritance issues loom large in many contexts and are one possible reason these young people want to know more about their biological fathers. I do not, however, believe that economic factors alone can explain this deeply felt yearning, which spans the literature on adoption in general *and* children born of wartime rape. Here it is fathering rather than parenting that seems to drive the desire for origins and a sense of loss and displacement. Indeed, Denov's findings illustrate that even those young adults who had a close relationship with their mothers also wanted to know more about their fathers and their heritage. Additionally, research "participants frequently mentioned that they had first heard about their origins through insults, comments, or stories told by family and community members."[52]

They crave the "truth," which may consist of confirming the whispers and insults. For some, the truth will be that their father was a violent member of the "enemy," a man who brutalized their mothers, leaving these young adults worried that perhaps they carry malevolent traces in their own bodies. For others, knowing the truth of their fathers will prompt them to feel greater sympathy for their mothers and to admire the strength required to raise a child under such conditions. Disclosure is akin to a pharmakon, offering both remedy and poison. And yet, when factoring in time depth, these two cases indicate that pain cedes to acceptance and to a greater understanding of oneself. This holds true for the young adults in both studies; it is less clear what the long-term impact is on their mothers. With these examples in mind, let us consider Colombia and the challenges of reparations for children born of wartime sexual violence.

Colombia: A Test Case

Colombia's civil war was the lengthiest armed conflict in the Western Hemisphere. What began six decades ago as a war waged by Marxist revolutionaries against an exclusive political system devolved into a bloody struggle over resources: military, paramilitary, guerrillas, domestic elites, and multinational actors have all vied for control of this resource-rich country. In the struggle, all groups committed serious human rights violations.

The FARC is Colombia's oldest and largest guerrilla group, established in 1964. From its beginnings as a primarily rural-based guerrilla movement, the FARC grew in both size and influence. With time, the Marxist ideology that had been a key component of its foundation ceded to a desire for territorial control and wealth. The FARC financed itself through kidnapping, extortion, drug trafficking, and drug trade protection. In the eyes of its critics, the FARC became one more violent armed actor rather than a revolutionary alternative.

The second-largest guerrilla movement is the Ejército de Liberación Nacional (ELN, National Liberation Army), which also began operations in 1964.

Unlike the rural FARC, the ELN was mostly an outgrowth of university unrest. The ELN's ideology, which has traditionally been considered a mixture of Cuban revolutionary theory with liberation theology, began calling for a Christian and Communist solution to the problems of poverty, political exclusion, and corruption. However, discourse and action again diverged as the ELN lost its focus and began engaging in illegal activities to finance its actions. At present the ELN has an estimated 3,500 to 4,000 combatants and since July 2004 has been engaged in sporadic peace negotiations with the Colombian government. As with the FARC, the ELN has appeared on the US list of terrorist organizations. And there is another group that was placed on that same list in September 2001: the paramilitaries.

The terms *paramilitary organization* and *self-defense group* have been used to describe a variety of armed groups over the past several decades. Paramilitary organizations have evolved considerably since the 1960s, when US military advisors first recommended the organization of "indigenous irregulars" as a fundamental component of the Colombian counterinsurgency strategy, then aimed at defeating leftist guerrilla movements.[53] Thus began the complicated relationship between the Colombian state, the US government, and the alternately legal and illegal armed groups known collectively as the paramilitaries. Although promoted as "self-defense committees" founded to protect local communities against the guerrillas, they came to assume greater responsibility in state-organized "search and destroy" operations seeking to eliminate the guerrillas. The use of paramilitaries as auxiliary forces assumed a central place in the government's counterinsurgency plan, and paramilitary groups would become regional elites' preferred option for protecting their interests and suppressing social protests. It was the fusion of paramilitary organizations and drug trafficking that gave rise to the phenomenon known as "paramilitarismo"—the transformation of paramilitary groups into an economic, social, and political force that infiltrated Colombian society.[54]

By the presidential elections of 2002, an increasing number of Colombians demanded change. The debacle of past peace processes readied many sectors of Colombian society for someone who would take a "heavy-handed" approach to the violence. Álvaro Uribe promised to be that man. President Uribe was not inclined to attempt dialogue with the FARC, whom he considered a "terrorist threat." Rather, Uribe cautiously explored the possibility of negotiating with the paramilitaries, while simultaneously promising to rein in the guerrillas. There was a certain irony to these negotiations: in part the paramilitary demobilization was an attempt to "deparamilitarize" the

Colombian state. Earlier government initiatives to fill its absence with civilian defense committees went beyond the state's control, so at some juncture the government was destined to find itself negotiating peace not only with the guerrillas but with the paramilitaries as well. The signing of the Santa Fe de Ralito I agreement on July 15, 2003, marked the beginning of formal talks between the government and paramilitary groups linked to the Autodefensas Unidas de Colombia (AUC, United Self-Defense Forces of Colombia). The terms of the agreement included the demobilization of all combatants by the end of 2005 and obligated the AUC to suspend its lethal activities, maintain a unilateral ceasefire, and aid the government in its anti-drug-trafficking efforts.

In addition to these initiatives, on July 22, 2005, President Uribe signed Law 975, the Justice and Peace Law. The law embodied the competing tensions of peace and justice, and victim-survivor's organizations succeeded in challenging certain key aspects of the law on the grounds that it failed to provide sufficient assurance of their right to truth, justice, and reparations. Under pressure from victim-survivor's organizations and domestic and international human rights organizations, the Colombian government was forced to modify the law; although still imperfect when measured by absolute human rights standards, the Colombian Constitutional Court ruling of May 2006 did serve to strengthen the law in response to these challenges. If at one time states wielded their sovereign prerogative to issue amnesties in the name of political expediency, stability, and peace—prerogatives that characterized past demobilization efforts in Colombia—changes in international norms increasingly place limits on the granting of leniency to perpetrators, forcing governments to address transitional justice topics such as truth, justice, and redress.

It was upon this terrain that the administration of President Juan Manuel Santos and the leadership of the FARC began their peace negotiations in 2012 in the Cuban capital, Havana. During preliminary discussions, the two sides agreed on six issues crucial to achieving a lasting peace: rural land reform, political participation for FARC ex-combatants once they laid down their weapons, the elimination of illicit drugs and drug trafficking, securing justice for victims of the conflict, negotiating the laying down of weapons by the FARC and subsequent reintegration of their rank and file into civilian life, steps for the implementation of the peace agreement and formal end to the conflict, and the establishment of a Commission for the Clarification of Truth, Coexistence and Non-Repetition, tasked with clarifying and establishing the truth about Colombia's armed conflict. All that remained was a referendum on the 297-page peace agreement. How hard could it be to "sell the peace" after a fifty-two-year war that had resulted in 220,000 people killed and another 50,000 disappeared, vast expanses of land grabbed up and some 5 million people internally displaced, and 8.2 million registered victims?

On October 2, 2016, Colombians (or at least 37 percent of them) headed to the polls to vote on the peace accords. The words on the ballot were straightforward: "Do you accept the final agreement to terminate the conflict and build a stable and lasting peace?" After a half century of armed conflict, it was almost inconceivable that anyone would vote No on this proposition— but they did. Sixty-three percent of the population abstained, some due to inclement weather, others due to apathy, and others (I suspect many) due to the prevailing sense that a Yes vote was virtually assured. Of the ballots cast, the outcome hinged on some fifty thousand votes in a country with fifty million people. The final tally was 50.2 percent versus 49.7 percent. The peace accords were voted down.

But for those Colombians who voted No, *what* were they saying no to? For some constituencies within the No camp, anything less than extended jail time for FARC combatants—especially commanders—was anathema. Although paramilitary leaders had been given drastically reduced prison sentences in exchange for offering "full confessions" about their violent activities, there was a sector of the population that could not abide any lenience with the FARC. This position, which I call "maximalist intransigence," resulted in Human Rights Watch (HRW) ending up on the side of a No movement composed of former president Álvaro Uribe and conservative factions of the Catholic and Evangelical Churches. However, the voting patterns indicate that Colombians living in those areas most impacted by the armed conflict voted Yes on the referendum, suggesting that victims of the conflict were embracing the peace accords not for their perfection but for their promise. Adding to this volatile mix were the "culture wars" that emerged around the time of the plebiscite and the moral panic generated around a possible erosion of "family values."

While the Colombian government and the FARC were negotiating in Havana, back in Bogotá the government released a new manual for public schoolteachers, with educational content designed to prevent the discrimination against and bullying of LGBTQ+ students. Education Minister Gina Parody, who is openly gay, was targeted by conversative forces and accused of attempting to "teach homosexuality" in the schools. This occurred against a wider backlash against feminist gains and gender studies more generally.

A cornerstone of feminist scholarship is the insistence that gendered identities are social creations rather than biological bedrocks. As obvious as this claim may be, it has met with vociferous attacks from conservative groups on the grounds that "gender ideology"—a term one can trace to anti-LGBTQ+ activists and conservative clergy in Europe—seeks to undermine "God-given" gender roles and traditional conceptions of the family. Uribe embraced these claims and in one tweet warned, "Saying that one is not born female or male, but that this is defined by 'society,' is an abuse of minors, a disrespect of nature and of the family."[35] For Uribe, who had always taken a close-fisted approach to the FARC, the elements were there to generate a strategic moral panic. He and his followers tied these proposed curricular reforms to provisions in the peace accords that were designed to promote gender equality and protect people of "diverse sexual orientation and identities." Uribe and his allies presented these parallel developments as a veritable siege on Colombian society, driving a media narrative that fueled conservative fears of sexual- and gender-based rights on the one hand, and the establishment of a legal scaffolding that would be too lenient with the FARC on the other. This made for a heady fusion: pamphlets promoting the No campaign included, "Colombia is in danger! Of falling under the control of a communist dictatorship and the imminent passage of a gender ideology."[36]

Shaken, President Santos sent his negotiating team back to Havana to revise the peace accords as quickly as possible. The revisions clarified certain legal issues with the FARC and included a "watering down" on gender issues to reflect more traditional ideas of womanhood and the family. This time around, President Santos did not risk another embarrassing defeat via plebiscite. The accords were fast-tracked and ratified by the Colombian Congress over protests from the Uribista factions. Moving from peace on paper to implementing the accords has posed many challenges in the polarized context of Colombia. One reason transitional justice processes are so challenging is that postconflict reckoning and accountability require more than the compilation of testimonies, the empathetic listening to narratives of suffering, and the rewriting of patently false histories of atrocity. It is necessary but insufficient to circulate previously silenced memories in the service of establishing shared truths about lengthy periods of lethal violence: coexistence requires the redistribution of resources, both symbolic and material. War does not only produce winners and losers, victims and perpetrators: it also produces benefactors who may have profited mightily from the suffering and economic dispossession of others. Colombia is a poignant case in point.

For more than five decades, Colombia has faced one of the world's most acute internal displacement problems associated with conflict and violence, illustrating that internal displacement can be a strategy of war rather than an unforeseen form of collateral damage. Various actors—including drug traffickers, cattle farmers, agrobusinesses, and paramilitaries—have participated in a massive "land grab," appropriating between 6.6 and 8 million hectares of land.[57] This "counteragrarian reform" has resulted in an estimated 5.9 million internally displaced people (IDPs), to use a humanitarian term.[58] The majority of these folks are Afro-Colombian, Indigenous, or peasant farmers.[59] In recognition that transitional justice measures must do something *for* victims and not simply *to* perpetrators, in 2011 former president Santos passed Law 1448, known as the Victims and Land Restitution Law. The law aimed to secure victims' rights to truth, justice, guarantees of nonrepetition, and some measure of reparations. Rhetoric aside, I consider this a neoliberal peace package that does not provide for radical transformations in the political and socioeconomic violence that continues to plague the country.

There is, however, an innovation that bears upon our discussion. The Victims and Land Restitution Law specifically recognizes children born of sexual violence as direct victims with a right to reparations, and it calls for children born of conflict-related sexual violence to be given the same level of reparations as direct victims of sexual violence. These children—many of whom are now young adults—are eligible to receive a trust fund in their name, consisting of thirty monthly salaries that they can access once they turn eighteen.

This decree was the topic of *vigorous* debate during my lectures and interviews in Colombia in 2019. How does one move from law into practice, given that many women have done everything humanly possible to make sure their children born of rape have no idea how they were conceived? Several women insisted they wanted to spare their children this painful information—spare them the transmission of their painful memories. The issue of disclosure is, once again, deeply fraught.

As the first reparations program to recognize children born of sexual violence as direct victims, there was no precedent for how to do this. The Victims' Unit—the state entity responsible for registering victims and disbursing reparations—struggled with questions such as whether the children or young adults would have to give their own declaration, or if the mother's declaration (should she choose to provide it) would be sufficient. The Victims' Unit ultimately decided to create two ways for children born of conflict-related sexual violence to access the reparations they are entitled to: they could either directly give their statement, or they could receive reparation if their mother provided a declaration in which she revealed the name of her child.

The next challenge was then how to distribute the reparations, and efforts to date have been roundly criticized. In some cases, children (now young adults) received a letter indicating that they would be receiving reparations because they were victims of sexual violence, with that letter serving as the first time they learned about the violent circumstances of their conception. This situation was more characteristic of urban areas, where migration during the violence provided some anonymity and made it easier to hide this information. In an urban context, it was more likely that these young people truly had no idea how they were conceived. As the Rwandan examples demonstrate, abrupt disclosure can be very traumatic, and the Victims' Unit had not provided counseling services to help people prepare to receive or to process this emotionally charged information. The mothers of those young people were livid, the process described as "revictimizing" to the women and damaging to their children.[60]

In other areas people knew (or at least suspected) that a child was born of sexual violence. I recall another mother, "Angela," a young Afro-Colombian woman who had been raped by a lighter-skinned member of the FARC. She lived in a small town and decided to tell no one—not her boyfriend, not even her mother—what had happened. Then the waiting began. One month, then six weeks, then two months, and still she did not menstruate. She hid her swelling belly as best she could and prayed: "Every day I prayed to God, please let this baby be black. Please God." Her prayers were not answered; she gave birth to a white baby boy. Everyone knew, and everyone gossiped until she left her small town for the city. Her son is grown now and has been a source of comfort for her. Indeed, she loves him. Even so, Angela lamented the life she had not led; as an adolescent she had planned to study hard and make something of herself. Those plans were thwarted by rape. A rape survivor's grief has many sources, and mourning lost plans and "a life not led" weighs heavily on a woman's heart.

Angela had left for the city, but not all women were able to do so. In certain Afro-Colombian regions, rape survivors and their children were forced to live among the gossip. Children with lighter skin were called "los blanquitos" (the little white ones), and people knew they were the result of rape by a member of the armed forces, paramilitaries, or the guerrillas. These public secrets have a different logic regarding disclosure but must still be handled with an understanding that confirmation of the unspoken or the whispered can also set painful processes into play.

Another disturbing element of the reparations program concerns poverty and consent. The mothers with whom I spoke were all of modest means, and the promise of financial reparations for their children weighs against their resistance to having their grown children learn how they were conceived. For women with limited financial resources, this choice is agonizing. For instance, "Paula" was deeply torn on this issue. She had spent her entire life ensuring that her daughter would never find out that her mother had been raped: "My daughter is happy, she has a good life. Why in the world should she have to know about this? I've done everything possible to make certain she never, ever found out." Being forced to choose between reparations for one's child and concerns about what this information might do to them is a moral dilemma that in itself may constitute a gendered harm.[61]

Reflecting on my conversations with Colombian mothers who gave birth as a result of wartime rape, two issues stand out. The first is sequencing, which is closely connected to the second: access to specialized psychological services. Until a woman has had the opportunity to address her own trauma, asking her to talk frankly with her child, of any age, can be painfully revictimizing. I suggest we think in terms of sequencing: working with sexual assault survivors who were impregnated as a result of that assault must take priority. Some women will choose to abort; some will choose to carry the fetus to term and then place the baby up for adoption; still others give birth and keep the baby. Each decision involves complicated emotions and requires support. This support requires more than "psychosocial activities."

I first encountered "psychosocial activities" when I began working with former combatants in Colombia. The Disarmament, Demobilization and Reintegration (DDR) program aimed to assist combatants in the transition to civilian life, and all beneficiaries were required to attend psychosocial workshops in order to remain in the program and receive a monthly stipend.[62] The incorporation of psychosocial activities was in line with the United Nations Department of Peacekeeping Operations (DPKO) and its 2010 guidelines for DDR best practices. The DPKO encouraged DDR practitioners to design and implement psychosocial interventions that "help individuals to regain their capacity for resilience, while restoring social capital and contributing to a greater sense of national unity," acknowledging that "efforts will be most effective when utilizing indigenous and local resources to develop, translate and communicate positive psycho-social messages."[63] The nod to psychosocial interventions was laudable, albeit vague. What exactly does the "psychosocial" entail? Who are its agents, and where does this psychosocial work occur? I found that most former combatants laughed at the mandatory psychosocial sessions, which seemed to involve techniques that could range anywhere from a short appointment with a therapist to attending a bake sale in a parking lot. They begrudgingly attended, while complaining that they were "totalmente psicosocializado" (totally psychosocialized), an assurance they offered in a tone vacillating between cynicism and lament.

I found myself hearing the same derisive comments from these mothers. One service the Victims' Unit provides are "psychosocial activities," and although they are well intentioned, they are not addressing the serious consequences of sexual assault, unwanted pregnancies, and forced maternity. One of the women rolled her eyes and asked what possible good it could do for her to close her eyes and imagine she hears the ocean waves. Another lamented that she was asked to "talk about her memories over and over." She shrugged. "It's nice, but what good is it doing me to keep talking about it?" What did she want? "Peer counselling with someone who understands what I am struggling with."

Sexual assault survivors may benefit from—and some may require—psychological services with specialized therapists. When we consider the consequences of sexual assault, we are faced with a list of possible sequelae: unwanted pregnancies, untreated sexually transmitted diseases, incontinence, scarring, fistulas, infertility, and trauma. These consequences require a sophisticated and comprehensive response. This response must be a priority, and then—perhaps then—women may be more inclined to speak with their children about what happened. The mothers were clear in asking for psychological assistance for themselves, and to prepare them for any conversations they might choose to have with their children. The emphasis: that conversation should be their choice.

The Colombian experience underscores the need to guarantee psychological accompaniment to the mother and her child. It also raises the question of what to do when the rights of children born of conflict-related sexual violence intersect or conflict with a mother's right to privacy. The competing rights regimes do not end with the birth of children born of rape: this is a source of ongoing tension. Ultimately, policy makers need to consider how they can deliver reparations to children born of conflict-related sexual violence in a way that does not harm them, that respects their mothers, and that helps them both become fully engaged in their families and communities.

A good place to start? The DPKO advocated attention to indigenous and local resources when planning psychosocial interventions. Setting aside my concerns that "psychosocial" can be a way to "deskill" mental health services, Colombia has an important resource that spans several generations of armed violence: from La Violencia of the 1950s into the present, armed conflict has included forms of sexual violence, unwanted pregnancies, and forced maternity. There must be several generations of children born of conflict-related sexual violence in the country—as well as mothers, families, and communities that have addressed this issue, even if only in whispers and strategic silences. What might they tell us about a half century and more of armed violence and its legacies? The mothers have a rallying cry: "Nada para nosotras sin nosotras" (Nothing for us without us). The literature on reparations indicates that the most successful programs involve the active participation of the victim-survivors themselves.[64] Convene the mothers who are willing to speak, and the grandmothers as well. Convene the now-adult children and listen to what they say about their lives and life chances. At each juncture, have specialized therapists and skilled peer counsellors ready to accompany people when they need support in sharing their painful histories. There is a wealth of expertise and information that has not yet been tapped; it is time.

2

SITUATED BIOLOGIES

My daughter was born the day after the massacre at Lloqllepampa. I was hiding in a hut. I had to throw my husband out because if the soldiers showed up, they would have killed him. I gave birth all by myself. During that time—when we were in hiding—I didn't even have milk for my baby. How could I have milk when there was nothing to eat? One day some other women told me, "If you leave your baby in the mountain, the *apu* [mountain god] would grab her and she would die." Remembering this, I left her on a mountain so that she would die. How was she going to live like this? I had passed on all my suffering through my blood, through my breast. I saw her from a distance, but since she was crying I had to go back and get her because if the soldiers heard her, they would have killed me. This is why I say that my daughter is still traumatized by everything that happened—everything that passed through my milk, my blood, my thoughts. Today, she can't study. She's seventeen years old and is still in fifth grade. She can't progress—every year she fails. She says she has a headache, that her head burns. What is it—fear? She's always been like this.

—SALOMÉ BALDEÓN, Accomarca, July 2001

It was 1995 when I began working in the highlands of Peru. Rural communities throughout Ayacucho were still in ruins: burned houses, abandoned farmlands, and innumerable mass graves converted the earth itself into yet another victim of the internal armed conflict. The social landscape was equally volatile as campesinos struggled to rebuild their communities in the shadow of a recent past marked by lethal, intimate violence. The memories were palpably fresh, painful, omnipresent; they settled in the mountains where so many had died, in the rivers tinged red by blood, and in the ruins that served as silent witnesses to the atrocities. But it was during conversations with Quechua-speaking women that other "historical sites" emerged: the women's own bodies, which incorporated these lacerating memories.

I began writing about those experiences in *Entre prójimos: El conflicto armado interno y la política de la reconciliación en el Perú.* Thinking about children born of wartime sexual violence sent me back to those conversations and field notes with a new set of questions about war, intergenerational trauma, and theories of transmission. There were detailed field notes from a long conversation in 1997 with a group of women in Umaru, a community that had been virtually destroyed during the war. I was seated with the women amid the burned-out remains of someone's home, conducting a health care needs assessment for an NGO. At one point during our conversation, I asked the women which health care services were a priority in their community. Past experience indicated that a question about services needed could solicit responses that ranged from livestock to food to materials to build an Evangelical church. The women murmured briefly among themselves, and finally one woman responded on behalf of the group: "What we need most are pills to make us forget." The women suffered from a variety of memory afflictions, and many wondered why they should remember everything that had happened when it only served to "martyr their bodies." Their memory afflictions did not merely index an internal world of private suffering but rather a social world that caused distress. The memory of unaddressed wrongs, of economic dispossession, of loved ones brutally killed—these memory afflictions indicted a social world that was capable of making people very ill indeed.

Among those afflictions were *mal de rabia* (the illness of rage, frequently linked to seeing the unpunished perpetrators and rapists living in their midst); *llakis* (toxic memories that swell inside the body); *regla blanca* (white discharge, resulting from chronic uterine or vaginal infections, one possible sequela of rape), and concerns about their breast milk and what it might do to their infants. Not only did toxic memories torment the women; they also posed a danger to their children.

Quechua speakers have elaborated a sophisticated theory regarding the transmission of suffering from mother to child, either in utero or via the mother's breast milk. The term *mancharisqa ñuñu* captures these intergenerational concerns. In Quechua, *ñuñu* means both breast and milk, depending on the context and the suffix, and *mancharisqa* refers to fear.

With the term *mancharisqa ñuñu*, women lamented what their breast milk might do to their babies in light of all they had seen, suffered, and survived. I sought to capture this double meaning: to capture how strong negative emotions can alter the body and how a mother could, via blood in utero or via breast milk, transmit this dis-ease to her baby. The best translation seemed to be "la teta asustada"—literally, the frightened breast.

Some years later, the film director Claudia Llosa read *Entre prójimos* and was equally moved by the women's narratives and concerns. Drawing upon the intergenerational transmission of fear and toxic memories, she wrote and directed the lyrically powerful film *La teta asustada* (The Milk of Sorrow). The film went on to win the 2009 Golden Bear Award at the Berlin International Film Festival and was nominated for the Best Foreign Film Oscar at the Academy Awards in 2010. In Peru, national pride in the first widely lauded Peruvian film battled with concerns from certain social sectors that people would think the country "primitive" or "backward" if they saw the film, which addressed sexual violence, racism, and poverty head on. The film included dialogue in Quechua, the beautiful yet internally devalued language of the country's Indigenous people: the film laid bare the deep cleavages between coastal elites and the urban and rural poor who endure ongoing ethnic discrimination. These gaps infused various reviews of the film, with a number of commentators referring to "la teta asustada" as an "ancient belief" or "Andean myth." "Belief" and "myth" leave little room to appreciate the sophisticated *theories* that Quechua speakers have elaborated about violence and its effects.

The film was screened in the Department of Ayacucho at a large public event in the central plaza of Huanta, hometown of the lead actress, Magaly Solier. Then the emails began to arrive. I was moved by the young adults who wrote to tell me, "I now understand why I am the way I am." The film helped them make sense of their chronic fear, sense of distrust and anxiety, and memories that plagued them—memories of a war they might not have lived but had experienced from within their mother's womb, or growing up listening to the stories their relatives told about the *sasachakuy tiempo* (the difficult years).

* * *

Among Native Americans, First Nations people, and Indigenous communities, the concept of historical or intergenerational trauma addresses the consequences of settler colonialism, massacres, genocidal policies, pandemics, forced relocation, and the prohibition of spiritual and cultural practices: in sum, "the additive effects of multiple traumatic events occurring over generations."[1] As Maria Yellow Horse Brave Heart has found in her sustained qualitative research with members of the Lakota Nation, historical trauma is attentive to the embodied burden of carrying an ancestral legacy of trauma.[2] One cornerstone of the concept turns on the intentionality of the violence, and the purposeful, destructive intent of the perpetrators.[3] The resonance of this theory across Native and Indigenous groups is significant and reminds us that bodies are historical processes and historical sites. The emphasis on the exposed and entangled relationship of the human and beyond-the-human offers a much-needed antidote to human exceptionalism and its devastating impact on this planet.

I consider various environments in my analysis and begin with the making of mothers into environments for fetuses, in this case under violent circumstances. My analysis is informed by years of working with Quechua-speaking communities in Peru and by the rich literature and theorizing produced by Native American scholars. I will also draw upon medical anthropology and the burgeoning field of epigenetics but begin by placing these approaches within the long theoretical traditions of Native American and Indigenous peoples. Kim TallBear has trenchantly critiqued settlers and scientists for "discovering" forms of Indigenous knowledge that were previously ignored or suppressed by colonialism, referring to these "discoveries" as a "Settler Epiphany."[4] It would not be news to a Quechua-speaking mother to be told her body and environment are coproduced, or that the "very substances of the world pass through her."[5] She already knows that, as do many other women raised with Indigenous epistemologies. Hence my insistence on *situating* epigenetics, "embedded bodies," "embodiment," and "situated biologies" within a lengthy genealogy of Indigenous and Native American theorizing on the human and more-than-human entanglements that shape the world.[6]

Patriarchal Biologies

War does not impregnate women, but men do. It is not only birth certificates and national identity documents that link the babies and children to their rapist fathers: theories of transmission are another sphere in which biological fathers, although physically absent, may be omnipresent in the symbolic register. Although DNA and genetic codes animate scientific discussions of inherited traits, there are other ways of theorizing the characteristics passed from parent to child via semen, blood, and breast milk or while in utero. Understanding these theories of transmission helps us understand how women may feel about the fetus growing inside them, and how the baby they birth will be viewed by their family and community.

When considering rape-related pregnancies, the primacy given to the biological father's seminal violence almost obscures the maternal contribution to the baby's identity. Across contexts, one can find examples of people's concern that the baby will be innately, biologically predisposed to violence, to seeking revenge, to literally embodying their father's malevolence. For example, Jennifer Scott was lead author of a qualitative study in the Democratic Republic of the Congo with fifty-five women who had become pregnant as a result of sexual violence. She was interested in determining the factors that influenced the women's decisions to abort or to carry the fetus to term, and she found that a key concern for the women was the biological identity of the father and what that would mean for the social reintegration of their child in the future. Among the women who chose to abort and were able to do so, patriarchal biology loomed large:

> I was so happy to get it terminated and I felt stable. I felt as if I carried a little devil in my womb. (sixty-year-old woman)

> I couldn't carry the pregnancy to term and deliver a child born from sexual violence. I thought he would behave like his father, the rapist. (twenty-five-year-old woman)[7]

Similarly, in Binaifer Nowrojee's powerful report *Shattered Lives: Sexual Violence during the Rwandan Genocide and Its Aftermath*, she notes the pervasive assumption that children born of rape are biologically associated with the "enemy" via their rapist fathers. This assumption may explain why male children born of rape seem to provoke more fear than do female children: the idea that boys will grow up to behave "just like their fathers" may result in greater discrimination against these boys, a possibility that calls for further research.

In Peru, the traits associated with children born of rape reflected political affiliations and communal divisions. In communities that had suffered mightily at the hands of the military, the children of soldier-rapists were more likely to be ridiculed and rejected. In contrast, I found that those villages that ascribed their losses to the Sendero Luminoso guerrillas affixed their concerns on children fathered by guerrilla members; those children were considered "naturally rebellious" and prone to causing problems within the community. Here we see that rejection can be the result of political divisions and alliances; the constant, however, is the centrality of the biological father in terms of the child's identity.

Patriarchal biology was painfully relevant in Bosnia and Herzegovina as well, where rape camps and ethnic cleansing merged. Feminists achieved a major victory in establishing that rape was an offense against women *as women* rather than merely serving as a violation of male property rights. How the victory unfolded, however, had some disturbing consequences. In her insightful analysis, Karen Engle has traced the key debates that drove feminists into contentious camps: one of those debates centered on "everyday rape" versus "genocidal rape."[8] As Engle notes, by insisting on the genocidal intent of rape, "both women's rights advocacy and the ensuing jurisprudence tended to reify ethnic difference, diminish women's capacity to engage in sexual activity with the 'enemy' during the war, and downplay the extent to which any but extraordinary women could be perpetrators in war."[9]

The elision of women's agency and the portrayal of all Bosnian Muslim women as rape victims did women a disservice, and I agree with much of Engle's argument. Where we part ways is in the experiential component of the rapes and the theories of transmission that were not simply an ethno-nationalist or feminist imposition.

Engle discusses the flawed logic behind raping women with the goal of "making Serbian babies," and throws out the idea that this was ordered, or that there was intent. From a logical perspective, one can agree with her argument—sperm did not swim up reproductive tracts with a national flag attached to their tails—and yet arrive at a different set of questions. Ethnic identities frequently become more rigid during armed conflict or may emerge as the result of a conflict in which people elaborate difference and "other" the enemy by summoning imagined biological differences. Theories of transmission, however, may predate any conflict by decades or centuries, and it is clear that at least some of the Bosnian rape survivors were horrified to be carrying a Serbian fetus. We may not endorse this patriarchal understanding of genetic descent, but if it is operative for the women being raped and for their families and communities, then we must acknowledge its influence and critique how it works to the detriment of the women and any babies they may birth.

In her comparative work on children born of rape in Bosnia and Rwanda, Patricia Weitsman considered these children as a prism for identity politics.

She situated the different uses of rape within the politics of identity, especially with regard to whether ethnicity is or is not determined by the father's bloodline.[10] During the Serbian rape campaigns, "the paramount assumption underpinning these policies [was] that identity is biologically and paternally given."[11] From this perspective, women were mere vessels for transmitting paternal identity, and these were occupied wombs. Reifying ethnic difference in order to claim rape as genocide virtually erased the mother's contribution to the child's identity; a victory in the legal realm served to reinforce a patriarchal theory of transmission rather than reject it. Challenging this framework might have assisted these women and their children in overcoming rejection within their families and communities in the aftermath of war.

Revisiting Strategic Pregnancies

I have been writing about sexual violence for a long time and have insisted on foregrounding women's protagonism in the face of brutality: mothers who sacrificed their bodies to save their daughters from rape; women who walked up steep hills to the military bases to search for detained loved ones, knowing the price they would pay in exchange for their freedom or for information about where the body had been dumped; mothers who engaged in transactional sex to feed hungry children. When women have spoken about rape, they located that violation within broader social dynamics. They detailed the preconditions that structured vulnerability and emphasized their efforts to minimize harm to themselves and to the people they cared for. With their insistence on context, women situated their experiences of sexual violence—those episodes of brutal victimization—within womanly narratives of heroism. When recalling those conversations, I find myself once again seated across from Edilberta Choccña Sanchez in Hualla. She had remained in her community during the war years. Hualla had been considered a militant Sendero Luminoso support base; thus when the soldiers arrived in Hualla, they came to "castigar el pueblo"—punish the town. After recounting in detail the massive sexual violence that had occurred in the military base, Choccña Sanchez took a deep breath, shook her head, and added in a voice resonant with admiration: "So much courage! Those women defended themselves with so much courage."

At times, women were confronted with alternatives that were all distasteful yet not uniformly wretched. The threat of sexual violence and pregnancy hovered over daily life. Recall Weitsman's observation: "Once born, the identity of war babies is inextricably linked to their rapist fathers."[12] Given the centrality of the father's identity in determining the fate of children born of wartime rape—whether through behavioral predispositions, ethnic identity, physical appearance, or some other characteristic—it was logical that women would make efforts to exert some control over their reproductive labor, and to break that inextricable link. "Strategic pregnancies" aimed to do just that—and more. According to Señora Tomayro of Hualla:

> The soldiers dragged my husband out of the house, dragged him to the plaza. Then they disappeared him. I followed them to Canaria to look for him. I demanded they give him back to me. Those soldiers beat me—my chest still aches from how they beat me. They wanted to abuse me, but they couldn't. After everything they did to me, I don't forgive them. It's their fault my children never went to school. Let them come here and at least fix my house! I have three children. After my husband disappeared—well, the soldiers wanted to abuse me. They tried to and I knew I didn't want to have a child from those devils. I decided it would be better to have the child of one of my paisanos. I had the child of a widower so I could make sure those miserable pigs didn't have that pleasure [of impregnating her]. They raped in groups—they raped in line. How could a woman tolerate so many men? Not even a dog could put up with it.

Señora Tomayro's words condense a great deal. Access to reproductive health care and family planning was minimal prior to the war and was further reduced by the destruction of hundreds of rural health posts during the internal armed conflict. Rape frequently resulted in unwanted pregnancies, which could bring further pain and rejection to the mother as well as to her child. Within a context of minimal choices—and even less recourse to contraception—women sought to exercise some control over their bodies, even if the range of control was reduced to strategically getting pregnant by a member of their community (a *comunero*) rather than by soldiers lined up for gang rape.

But there is more. Women were somehow trying to preserve "community," which confers both rights and obligations. Single mothers complain about the challenges of forcing the fathers of their children to recognize the child and provide the mother with some sort of financial assistance. This struggle plays out in every community. However, by giving birth to a *comunero*'s baby, women bring that child into a familial and communal network of reciprocity and obligation. Becoming pregnant by a *comunero* affords the woman some means of assuring she has someone against whom she can press her claims and those of her child.

Yet this is not just about material resources; it is also about the emotional toll. The faces of children conceived through rape will serve as reminders to their mothers of a painful past. These strategic pregnancies are protective and preventive. They are women's efforts to exert some control over the present as well as the future, over their bodies and the production of "future memories." Women like Señora Tomayro were trying to make their fetuses bearable.

In the years since I first wrote about Señora Tamayro, I have been asked if it is true that the widower next door was the biological father of her baby. Perhaps we do not need to know the truth but do need to understand the social logics that motivated her and the widower. He had grown children, but some had been killed in combat and others had migrated to the capital city of Lima in search of economic opportunities. They established their own families there and preferred the amenities of urban life. Although they occasionally sent him a package, their visits had waned to such a point that they rarely attended the community's annual celebration. He was alone and in his fifties—elderly by rural standards. Who would care for him when fetching water and firewood became arduous chores? Without children to care for him, he would join the millions of elderly people in this world who are left with no "safety net" when old age settles into their bones. If indeed Señora Tomayro had spun a useful fiction, it was one that served them both. Together they conceived a future, and no one else needed be the wiser.

Unbearable

One of the earliest articles about children born of wartime rape was R. Charli Carpenter's 2000 piece in *Human Rights Quarterly*.[13] I admire her for calling attention to this complex issue and disagree with some of her claims and positions. She states her wish to avoid a discussion of abortion.[14] I cannot. She also claims, with regard to Bosnia, that "in fact not all of the children were abandoned by their mothers or the Muslim community, though certainly the majority were. *The focus of feminist writing is on the ideal-type raped woman who hates her child, not on those who choose to raise their children. This is in keeping with the mainstream (and statistically inaccurate) notion in Western abortion-rights discourse that a raped woman never wants to raise her child.*"[15] There is no research cited to substantiate this totalizing claim, a spurious one to my mind.

Reproductive justice, a term and a movement developed by African American women in the United States, captures the range of choices that should be available to *all* women.[16] Against the backdrop of slavery, massive sexual violence, enforced sterilization campaigns, and the sustained assault on family life, African American women have articulated a broader perspective on reproductive justice advocacy that has challenged reproductive oppression. As they have argued, for Indigenous women and women of color, it is important "to fight equally for (1) the right to have a child; (2) the right not to have a child; and (3) the right to parent the children we have, as well as to control our birthing options, such as midwifery. We also fight for the necessary enabling conditions to realize these rights." The women have explicitly contrasted the reproductive justice framework with the "singular focus on abortion by the pro-choice movement."[17] This articulation of a full range of rights, coupled with the conditions that allow women to realize these rights, is precisely what feminist ethnographers of postconflict reconstruction should endorse. There is no side-stepping abortion and no foreclosing the other options women may choose or be forced to select. This is true for countries at peace, and perhaps even more so when considering war and its legacies.

I have sought to capture the *cultural meaning* of rape and other forms of sexual violence; as anthropologist Paul Richards has argued, "Ethnography is a tool to probe the social content of war."[18] Listening to *how* women speak about sexual violence is revealing. For example, in one highland Peruvian village, my colleagues Edith Del Pino and Leonor Rivera noted that women consistently referred to the soldiers as "animals." While this may at first seem nothing more than a standard wartime form of discursive dehumanization, attentiveness to language use is important. Women could have called the soldiers many things, so why "animals"? Del Pino and Rivera learned that the soldiers sodomized many of the women in this community, frequently in public venues in front of their family members and the broader community. The soldiers would subsequently strut through the streets, indicating which woman "ya está rota" (is already broken). The women in this community made clear that anal intercourse is not an acceptable form of sexual activity for them; indeed, they insisted that only "animals have sex that way," and that God considers it sinful for human beings to engage in such practices. The women's shame extends beyond their loved ones; they fear they are degraded sinners in the eyes of God. How would it be possible to respond to women's experiences of violence without listening to what they articulate as the gravest harm?

Another powerful example comes from research in Rwanda. Maggie Zraly, Sarah Rubin, and Donatilla Mukamana researched maternal resilience among survivors of rape that occurred during the genocide. Mothering was a potential source of strength, although "the relationships between mothers and children born from genocide-rape were particularly fraught with agonizing emotion."[19] One woman told the researchers that she had been gang-raped, adding that "sometimes you could be raped by one man and this was not very problematic. *It was the way I was raped that disturbs me.*"[20] Just as the form of sexual violence may be experienced as extraordinary, women may consider conflict-related rape pregnancies as also lying outside the framework of a "normal," albeit unwanted, pregnancy. For instance, I have mentioned the work of Jennifer Scott and her colleagues, who studied decision-making among rape survivors in the Democratic Republic of the Congo. Religious beliefs were one factor that influenced women's decisions with regard to terminating their pregnancies; however, even though women were influenced by Catholic prohibitions on abortion, "there were women who reported termination of the pregnancy in order to ensure their future well-being and who expressed that the termination of SVRPS [sexual-violence related pregnancies] should be considered differently than the termination of other pregnancies, which has important programming and policy implications."[21] Once again, women are articulating forms of violence and its consequences that lie outside prior norms and gender regimes.[22] As Elisabeth Wood has noted, "repertoires of violence" may magnify existing patterns of interpersonal violence; they may also reflect innovation as perpetrators begin deploying forms of violence that are truly unprecedented in a particular region or armed conflict.[23]

Is there something exceptional about the experience of conflict-related rape and pregnancy? Do these violations fall within a continuum of violence, or are they best understood as limit experiences that test the moral and perceptual imagination? Are people confronted with the massification of preexisting practices, or with forms of violence that reflect innovation and challenge the belief that violence has a limited range of manifestations?

A key figure in questioning the strengths and weaknesses of the "continuum of violence" approach is Margaret Urban Walker:

> The emphasis on a continuum of violence has indispensable uses. It is a basis for predicting forms of violence and harm women are likely to suffer, and it is essential to understanding social, institutional, and legal reforms needed in the aftermath of violence in conflict. Even

so, it does not adequately capture the experience of catastrophic and life-changing violence many women experience in these conflict situations. In the context of reparations, a focus on the victim's experience of harm and loss is essential.[24]

Thus, as useful as the continuum approach may be for capturing the "dailyness" of gendered and structural forms of violence, I share Urban Walker's insistence that we focus on how victim-survivors experience periods of armed conflict, and how they prioritize both the suffering they have endured as well as the forms of redress that might help them set their worlds right. When women, and other genders, insist they have experienced or witnessed forms of violence they never could have imagined—forms of violence that challenge any notion of a moral community with its capacity to impose limits on human action—then researchers and practitioners must acknowledge world-rupturing events.

* * *

Limit experiences, troubling theories of transmission, and concerns about assuring a bearable future: this is a volatile list of stressors, and *some* women will seek to terminate their pregnancies. Outlawing safe and accessible abortions will not stop them; it *will* cause some women to resort to methods that are potentially life-threatening for them and that in turn may result in the infliction of damage to the fetuses they unsuccessfully attempted to abort. The concatenation of violent conceptions, botched abortions, and birth defects warrants further research.

I found no systematic study of this connection; however, across a variety of postconflict settings, there is the recurrent theme of disabilities among children born of rape. For example, Carpenter noted that a number of children born to rape survivors in Bosnia were disabled, "although it is uncertain whether the factors relating to the rape itself were primarily responsible."[25] I suspect that at least some of those disabilities were the result of women's desperate efforts to abort their fetuses. In their survey article on the research and treatment of children born of rape, Elisa Van Ee and Rolf Kleber observe that "the exact effects of unsuccessful abortions on the child are unknown."[26]

In Peru, some women tried to abort with herbs, attempting to rid their bodies of fetuses they could not bear. While some women attempted to abort on their own, others sought out *curanderos* (healers) who used various abortifacients to perform *limpiezas* (cleansings). In this instance, the word *limpieza* is a form of veiled speech that allows women to maintain a useful ambiguity. Limpiezas of various sorts are quite common for a range of illnesses; it was only with time that my colleagues and I realized the women had visited *curanderos* to cleanse themselves literally—they complained of feeling filthy as a result of being raped—as well as to cleanse their uteri of unwanted pregnancies.

Still others resorted to infanticide. There is a long-standing practice of "letting die" those babies who are unwanted, perhaps because they are born with birth defects or are the product of rape. The idea is that *criaturas* (little babies) do not suffer when they die; one can leave them sleeping "mouth down," gently drifting off to death. Additionally, given women's concerns about the transmission of *llakis* (toxic memories) and *susto* (soul loss due to fright) from mother to baby, either in utero or via their mother's "milk of pain and sorrow," concerns about damage to their infants were omnipresent. How could a baby born of such suffering and fear be normal? Many women were certain they could not. Letting these babies die reflected a desire to spare them the violence of memory—and to spare their mothers these memories of violence.

In the Democratic Republic of the Congo, Scott and her colleagues found that many of the rape survivors with whom they worked felt an alienation from the fetus as well as from their own bodies. This alienation prompted some women to turn to "unsafe termination," which included traditional herbs, quinine tablets, and unspecified oral medications.[27] The same authors asked women in the pregnancy termination group "whether they considered continuing the pregnancy and if they could identify anything that would have made it easier for them to continue the pregnancy and raise the child."[28] The question that was *not* asked: *What would have made termination safer and easier?*

Side-stepping abortion in publications, policies, research, and interventions does a gross disservice to rape survivors and to the children they may unsuccessfully try to abort. The global gag rule, also known at the Mexico City policy, is the United States' antiabortion policy that prevents foreign organizations that receive US global health assistance from providing information, referrals, or services for legal abortion or advocating for access to abortion services in their country—even with their own money. The global gag rule was first introduced by President Ronald Reagan in 1984. Following the Reagan administration, the United States Agency for International Development (USAID) has enforced the policy during all subsequent Republican administrations and has rescinded the policy at the direction of all Democratic administrations. The global gag rule is part of a two-pronged approach to limiting abortion, working in tandem with the Helms Amendment.

Introduced by conservative senator Jesse Helms in 1973, the Helms Amendment was passed as a permanent part of the United States Foreign Assistance Act and has been in effect ever since. Despite the clear intent to be a limitation on abortion funding for family planning purposes, it has been interpreted and enforced as an outright ban on funding abortion for any reason—even in cases of rape, incest, and threat to a woman's life.[29]

The role of the United States in limiting access to abortion has a ripple effect: it is possible to attend conferences about children born of wartime rape and hear virtually no discussion of reproductive rights in general and abortion in particular. During my last trip to Colombia, I was invited to give two talks about children born of wartime rape. The second lecture was for government officials, representatives of NGOs, members of the armed forces, and UNICEF—in short, a wide swath of service providers and policy makers. Shortly before the event began, a Colombian colleague leaned in to whisper in my ear. Representatives of USAID sent her to request that I not talk about abortion. The global gag rule and the Helms Amendment have affected more than the family planning sphere; they also limit public debate and, perhaps, the very questions researchers believe they can ask.

* * *

> The soldiers, the Sinchis, came into the room [where she was detained]. All night they beat me, mistreated me. Then they began to abuse me, to rape me. Seven of them raped me. One came in, the other left, another came in. All night long. After that I wanted to kill myself, I wanted to die. I became pregnant. I thought that inside me, the product of all that, so many of them—it will be a monster. Oh, so many of them abused me! I thought I had a monster inside. What kind of thing could it be? What was growing inside me?
>
> —GEORGINA GAMBOA GARCÍA, testimony, Peruvian TRC's public hearing, Huamanga, April 8, 2002

I now consider two other trajectories: pregnancies resulting from gang rape, and children who were in utero when their mothers were raped. Recall the woman who insisted that it was the way she was raped that disturbed her, or Señora Tomayro, who was disgusted by the soldiers raping in groups, standing in line. People have theories of transmission regarding children conceived via rape; one can reasonably assume there are also theories regarding the consequences of gang rape, a form of sexual violence in which *one* biological father may not be identifiable. For Gamboa García, the fact that there were "so many of them" led her to worry about the "monster" growing inside her. The question she posed to herself was *"what* was growing inside me," not *"who."* Her concerns were not unique.[30]

Women in Ayacucho did talk about the legacies of gang rape, which was strongly associated with the armed forces. They were worried about how many heads and appendages the baby would have, given that so many men had been involved in its violent conception. The paternal contribution was once again given primacy and, in this case, literally assumed monstrous proportions. Is this true in other parts of the world? One cannot know from the current literature, but perhaps we can extrapolate from the women who have insisted that a rape-related pregnancy is *different from other pregnancies.*

Some women were already pregnant when they were raped during Peru's internal armed conflict. When I first began thinking about children born of wartime rape, I returned to volume 6 of the Peruvian Truth and Reconciliation Commission's *Informe Final* and to the chapter "Violencia sexual contra la mujer" (Sexual violence against women). In that chapter alone, there are thirty-seven references to girls and women who were impregnated as a result of wartime rape or exploitative sexual relationships. In most cases, these are third-party reports, and the women speaking refer to the phenomenon of unwanted pregnancies in the plural. "Salían embarazadas," "resultaron embarazadas"—the army, the police, and guerrillas of Sendero Luminoso and the Movimiento Revolucionario Túpac Amaru (Tupac Amaru Revolutionary Movement) are all named in the women's testimonies about rape-related pregnancies.

The PTRC does acknowledge that these children may suffer as a result of their origins:

> There are numerous cases of women who, being pregnant, were subjected to sexual violence and saw their pregnancies interrupted as a result of that violence. On the other hand, there are abundant cases of women who became pregnant as a result of the sexual violence they suffered at the hands of agents of the conflict; they found themselves obligated to assume a forced pregnancy and their children still continue to suffer the consequences of the violence.[31]

The reader is left with no further information about what those consequences might be and with great curiosity about the other trajectories hinted at in this paragraph. The women do indicate that the guerrillas frequently forced the girls and women to have abortions, and in those instances in which pregnancies were somehow carried to term, the babies were "forcefully taken away."[32] We do not hear more about the women who miscarried as a result of the sexual violence but can imagine how emotionally and physically wrenching that must have been. And what of those fetuses that survived the raping? One woman described the children she knew. Her village had been the site of a bloody massacre as well as sustained sexual violence:

> There are lots of sick children here—some are already adolescents. My neighbor's son is already a young man. When his mother was pregnant, the soldiers abused her. The boy was mistreated even before he was born! He was born different. Halfway *sonso* [senseless]. He can't speak. It's like he's crazy. It's as though he lost his use of reason. He doesn't talk, he's different—*sonso*. He's not like a normal child.

Given the brutality of the sexual violence reported in women's testimonies, one can assume these babies were beaten, indeed bludgeoned, during their mother's torture. Although it is unclear if these children experienced rejection, it *is* clear that mothers worried about the damage done to their babies during these violent sexual assaults. In addition to possible congenital defects, there were concerns that these children would be prone to epileptiform illnesses and intellectual disabilities, and would be born "sin la capacidad de querer" (without the capacity to love).

What does it mean for a child to be born without the capacity to love? One cornerstone of a child's emotional education in Quechua-speaking communities consists of "kuyachicuyta yachana"—learning how to make other people love you. Oh, how often mothers tell their children they need to learn how to make other people love them. This challenges the notion that motherly love is innate and simply waiting for a baby upon which to fixate.[33] Not all children are equally loved, even by their own mothers; women were candid in discussing which child they loved the most and which ones they did not.

What of the mother who finds herself unable to love a child born of rape? As one rape survivor in Rwanda lamented, "When people kill your family and then rape you, you cannot love the child."[34] Another woman insisted that for their mothers, "these are complicated children."[35] How could it be otherwise? For the mother who cannot love the fetus growing inside her, and for the fetus that inhabits that hostile environment, might it be that alienation begins in the womb? The literature on the importance of being held and loved as a baby is vast; what do we know about prenatal alienation? How can we discuss this possibility without, once again, asking women to hold up the entire sky?

Donna Haraway has asked, "What happens when human exceptionalism and bounded individualism, those old saws of Western philosophy and political economics, become unthinkable in the best sciences, whether natural or social? Seriously unthinkable: not available to think with."[36] She is underscoring the porosity, the exposure, of being and our ontological entanglement with the environment, composed of the human and more-than-human actors with whom we share this world.[37] When it comes to the maternal environment, we cannot think seriously with those old saws. Doing so slides too easily into blaming individual women for the outcomes of their pregnancies, obscuring the violent and perhaps toxic environments in which those women dwell.[38]

Indigenous communities have long insisted that the human body is intimately connected with both the land and the other life-forms that populate the world. In "Violence on the Land, Violence on Our Bodies: Building an Indigenous Response to Environmental Violence," a Mohawk midwife explains that in the Mohawk language, one word for midwife is *iewirokwas*, which means "she's pulling the baby out of the Earth."[39] There is an understanding of the human body as exposed and, given the impact of environmental racism on Indigenous and Native American communities, that exposure may mean that "each succeeding generation inherits a body burden of toxic contaminants from their mothers. In this way, we, as women, are the landfill."[40] This theoretical line of thinking predates and is complementary to recent theoretical turns in epigenetics, material feminisms, environmental humanities, and medical anthropology. The synergy can be electric.

Exposures

One can still visit the National Human Genome Research Institute's website and read the breathless wonder with which the Human Genome Project (HGP) was described as "one of the great feats of exploration in history. Rather than an outward exploration of the planet or the cosmos, the HGP was an inward voyage of discovery led by an international team of researchers looking to sequence and map all of the genes—together known as the genome—of members of our species, *Homo sapiens*. Beginning on October 1, 1990, and completed in April 2003, the HGP gave us the ability, for the first time, to read nature's complete genetic blueprint for building a human being."[41] Hailed at the time for having written the Book of Life, hindsight suggests that the HGP was a Cliff Notes version.[42] More recent developments question the genetic determinism associated with the HGP, with researchers from various fields asserting that there are multiple mechanisms of inheritance, such that biology must be understood as situated within sociohistorical contexts.[43] With terms such as "situated biologies," "embedded bodies," and "embodiment," anthropologists and social epidemiologists join epigeneticists in offering conceptual tools to grasp how life leaves its signature upon the body.[44]

Epigenetics is a burgeoning area within postgenomic life sciences research, and it focuses on how experiences, exposures, and environments alter gene expression. For example, DNA methylation is an epigenetic mechanism used by cells to control gene expression, akin to a signaling device that can fix genes in an on or off position. Thus DNA does not define a preordained nature but responds to a complex combination of nature *and* nurture. This is one way the world in which we live "gets under our skin": epigenetics situates the material body in time and space and, suggestively, within generational contexts as well.[45]

Among the classic intergenerational studies, war looms large (although children born of wartime rape are largely absent). In his review article "The Embodiment of War: Growth, Development, and Armed conflict," Patrick Clarkin explores the myriad pathways through which war becomes embodied and transmitted. He discusses the classic studies—the Dutch Hunger Winter, Holocaust survivors and their children, "bomb ecologies," among others—that suggest war creates a "suite of stressors" that may alter gene expression and create a "biological memory" that may linger long after war has subsided.[46] Among the intergenerational sequelae, one finds increased rates of anxiety, depression, stunting, asthma, and chronic heart disease. The timing of exposure is especially important; as Clarkin notes, "Depending on local circumstances, a developing embryo, infant, or child growing up in a place embroiled in armed conflict is likely to face—directly or indirectly—various stressors, including malnutrition, infectious disease, and/or psychological stress."[47] War can make for a toxic environment, and rape followed by forced pregnancy can in turn make the maternal environment inhospitable.

The insistence on exposure and environment presents great promise and lurking peril. In her trenchant critique of maternal-fetal epigenetic research, Sarah Richardson questions the centrality of maternal bodies as sites of epigenetic transmission and intervention. She cautions that the explanatory landscape of postgenomic sciences virtually excludes men and the paternal effects, while focusing on the maternal body as an "epigenetic vector" in ways that are redolent with traditional forms of determinism and reductionism.[48]

Given that the reproductive subject remains overwhelmingly female, this research could be marshalled in the service of reproductive *governance* rather than reproductive *justice*.[49] If the environment that is made to matter leads to a myopic focus on the womb and its (dis)contents, the peril lies in obscuring the multiple environments in which conception and reproductive labor unfold.

Morgan Hoke and Thomas McDade provide a useful antidote to uterine myopia. They suggest a rethinking of the "maternal environment," emphasizing that it is "a complex intergenerational set of physiological, social and political-economic processes rather than something that emerges in each body de novo."[50] This reorientation accounts for the historicity of bodies and for the embodied burden of war, toxic contaminants, discrimination: in sum, it accounts for exposures that are "terribly uneven, across such simultaneously social and material categories as class, race, and the disparities between the global north and the global south."[51] If this framework shapes feminist ethnographies of postconflict reconstruction, perhaps our work could more fully illuminate the fallacies of placing sole responsibility for pregnancy outcomes (or terminations) on those women who were violently made into "maternal environments."

I place this framework in dialogue with Michelle Murphy's concept of "distributed reproduction," which "sees questions of reproduction in infrastructures rather than only in the body in pregnancy, birth or infancy." The infrastructure under consideration includes "state, military, chemical, agricultural, economic, architectural; [the myriad actors] that assist, alter, rearrange, foreclose, harm and participate in the process of creating, maintaining, averting and transforming life in intergenerational time."[52] This wider lens accounts for the many forces that lie beyond any individual woman's control yet impact all her productive and reproductive labors. Perhaps this could respond to a common refrain that drew emphatic nods from the Colombian mothers who spoke about their children born of wartime rape: abort the baby, birth the baby, raise the child, or put it up for adoption, love that child or hate it—"no importa lo que pase, todo el mundo echa la culpa a la madre" (no matter what, everyone blames the mother).

3

ECOLOGIES AND AFTERMATHS

After official victory has been declared, how do we track the persistence of unofficial hostilities in the cellular domain, the untidy, attritional lethality that moves through the tissue, blood, and bone of combatants and noncombatants alike, moving through as well the living body of the land itself?

—ROB NIXON, *Slow Violence and the Environmentalism of the Poor*

Years ago, a student made a remarkable comment in one of my classes. We were discussing mass atrocity and genocide and the various ways that techniques of violence travel. At one point we read about the massacre of the Herero by German forces in the early 1900s and the treatment, primarily, of those women and children who survived the initial slaughter. They were forced into concentration camps, where almost 75 percent of those prisoners died from malnutrition and the impact of hard labor. We then moved on to the Holocaust, and once again to the concentration camps. The semester concluded by considering the history of settler colonialism in the United States and the reservation system, and with a set of readings about Jim Crow laws, mass incarceration, and racism. Hannah commented: "You know, I think one way power works is by distracting us, by keeping us from seeing the connections between things that happen at a distance in time and space." If power works by presenting phenomena as discontinuous, thereby distracting us from underlying logics and continuities, perhaps there is power to be reclaimed by tracing the proverbial dots and connecting seemingly disparate categories of events, and of being, that undergird human exceptionalism and its devastating impact.

In their thoughtful article about the Anthropocene and Indigenous philosophies, Heather Davis and Zoe Todd argue that the concept of the Anthropocene is grounded in a "logic of the universal" that situates a Eurocentric narrative as the privileged story that is told about our current environmental crisis as well as the place of humanity in that narrative.[1] The partitioning of life-forms into distinct and bounded categories—coupled with a taxonomical hierarchy of value—partakes of a colonial logic that positions some critters and territories as resources rather than co-inhabitants of this planet.[2] What is erased are histories of the world that existed and exist outside the history of predatory capitalism and its tools of dispossession and accumulation. One scholar who eloquently tells those other histories is anthropologist Kim Tall-Bear. As she has written, "Our genocide in the Americas included and continues to include our other-than-human relatives . . . kin we need to survive."[3] Countering this ongoing genocide and ecocide will entail, in part, addressing the impact of settler colonialism and its progeny, petrocapitalism and other extractive industries, which have severed the "relations between humans and the soil, between plants and animals, between minerals and our bones."[4]

Other agents in (literally) exploding those relationships are militarization and war. Recall the rivers of blood and the mass graves in the Peruvian highlands, converting the landscape into both a witness and a survivor of armed violence. Or consider Agent Orange and the "slow violence" it unleashed on bodies and landscapes.[5] Connecting events and beings across time and space: temporal proximity is too brief a time frame to capture the long-reaching legacies of militarization and armed conflict, and official body counts may be deceptive. Certain forms of violence will fall outside the time frame of "armed conflict" and will occur in locations not declared "war zones." They will also be inflicted on beings not considered human. And yet, what of those casualties? What of river-life-ways that are threatened?

It is appropriate to begin this exploration in Urabá, a microcosm of Colombia's past and present violence. My field notes are filled with a line repeated in conversations with locals: "This war begins and ends in Urabá." Whether or not that will prove to be a historical truth—the violence continues, taking on new forms, while recycling familiar actors—Urabá encompasses the contradictions, conflicts, abundant resources, and abject poverty that centuries of internal colonization, violent accumulation and dispossession, and racism can produce. When the Colombian Constitutional Court declared in 2016 that the region was the site of a "humanitarian, social and environmental crisis without precedent," this was not hyperbole but a long-standing truth. The language of crisis, however, risks erasing the centuries of racialized plunder that have been part of governing the region and its inhabitants.[6]

Urabá is located in northwestern Colombia and is characterized by a diversity of, well, diverse forms. In addition to being one of the most biodiverse territories in the country, it is also inhabited by multiple ethnic and racial groups: the population of approximately 500,000 is composed of Afro-Colombians (87 percent), Indigenous people (10 percent), and mestizo peasant farmers (3 percent).[7] For some the region is their ancestral home, while for others it was the promise of a better life—and a plot of arable land—that drew them to Urabá and to the Atrato River basin. Along the riverbanks, Afro-Colombian and Indigenous communities as well as peasant farmers have supported themselves by agriculture, artisanal mining, hunting, and fishing.

The Atrato River is the one of the longest in Colombia and arguably the most polluted. Its winding pathway begins high in the Western Andes mountain range, making a steep 416-mile descent into the Gulf of Urabá and, ultimately, into the Caribbean Sea, close to Panama. That sinuous path connects different beings, from blades of grass to aquatic birds; from *Trachemys medemi* turtles to human toddlers; from paramilitaries to guerrillas to displaced civilians. Stretches of the river have been dredged, contaminated by large-scale mining, deforested by illegal logging activities, while others have burned out and been bombed by the various armed actors for whom the land and water have value, while the inhabitants are cheap labor at best, human surplus at worst.

Time to travel the ebbs and flows of the Atrato and to trace an extended war story that winds its way upriver and back down to one feverish baby, with a few stops along the way. I begin by asking *who* and *what* counts as a war casualty. We will conclude with an expanded definition of both who and what, and ethnographic material with which to articulate environmental and posthumanist conceptions of justice.

The Atrato: A River with Rights

I first visited Colombia in July 2001, meeting up with two colleagues who also conduct research on armed conflict and peace building. We decided to head to Urabá, a northwestern region that straddles the departments of Choco and Antioquia. María Cristina at the UN office was a good contact, and we had heard that a number of forcibly displaced people had organized as Peace Communities and returned to their land.[8]

Urabá is rich in natural resources and man-made woe. National and international companies have amassed great wealth via the logging trade and the cultivation of bananas. Indeed, the region has been marked by cycles of violent extraction: of timber, gold, bananas—and people. The border with Panama serves as the thin line through which drugs are smuggled out and arms smuggled in. These resources, combined with the Atrato River and the port at Turbo, made control of this region desirable to international businesses and local elites as well as to the paramilitaries and the FARC who were engaged in a struggle for control of the region. At that point, the paramilitaries controlled the towns and cities in alliance with local elites and their military connections, and the guerrillas dominated the countryside.

As the violence escalated dramatically in the mid-1990s, thousands of people were forcibly displaced, leaving abandoned villages in their wake.

Atrato River, 2021

Crowding into the small towns along the Atrato as well as the larger cities of Turbo and Apartadó, peasants endured several years "andando en tierra ajena" (wandering in foreign land). The wandering caused these peasant farmers to begin organizing, motivated by their desire to return to land they had worked since the time of their great-grandparents—since a time before individual memory, a time passed down in the communal histories that tied generations of villagers to the great expanse of banana trees that grow bright green from the deep chocolate soil.

Villagers sought out the Catholic Church, turning to an institution that had an established presence in the region and enjoyed a degree of moral authority the Colombian government could only envy. The local diocese was personified by Father Leonides; whenever I asked someone to point me in the direction of the church, I found him. Father Leonides was a big man, in size and presence. There was nothing of the dour priest about him; rather, he ate with great appetite, enjoyed a good glass of Chilean wine, and, while his eyes may have been on heaven, his feet were firmly planted on the ground, in this world and its many problems.[9]

In the midst of his busy schedule, Father Leonides made time to explain the context in which the Peace Communities had been formed. His twenty years in Urabá gave Father Leonides an understanding of the violence that predated drug trafficking and arms smuggling.

> It is the cattle ranchers who have financed the violence in Urabá. They supported and nurtured the paramilitaries to push peasants off their land and to stop unions that might oppose them. In the mid-1990s the paras entered with force, and they accused these campesinos of being guerrilla sympathizers. The FARC had controlled this land for twenty years and had a coexistence [*convivencia*] with the campesinos. Yes, there was a relationship; campesinos paid their "vaccination" and lived with the presence of the FARC. But the paras accused these people of being guerrillas. The accused were in great danger—there was an exodus of thousands of people. In the Church we had to ask ourselves, "What response do we have?" We began building shelters for the displaced, but they dreamed of returning to their land. So there was a process of organizing to resist the violence. The Peace Communities were forged in that juncture. The campesinos came together to reclaim the possibility of life in these villages. The armed groups refer to the dead as the "quotas of war," and these campesinos were tired of filling those quotas.

As he spoke about the founding of the fifty-nine Peace Communities four years earlier, Father Leonides grew increasingly animated: "What these campesinos have organized is a truly revolutionary alternative—peace." He insisted that national efforts to negotiate peace would not resolve the regional issues that had fueled the war. Father Leonides maintained that peace would come from a series of regional peace processes and local initiatives. As he asked rhetorically, "Why do we think that armed actors are the ones who will bring peace to Colombia?"

A review of the accords the campesinos drew up reveals that the Peace Communities represented both a citizen initiative and a demand. Anyone who has ever worked with campesinos has heard them speak about their villages, and themselves, as "los olvidados"—the forgotten ones. They are referring to a geography of difference that informs the distribution of poverty, the administration of (in)justice, and the right to be considered citizens of the nation and not merely "wards of the state." But the "forgotten ones" also reflects what Colombian anthropologist Diana Bocarejo has called "a longing for the state."[10] In fact, one clause in the accords demanded the unarmed presence of the Colombian state, in the form of services, public works, and the fulfillment of the state's obligations to its citizenry. As one of the campesinos who participated in drafting the agreements explained, "We are no government pilot project. The Colombian state has never treated campesinos as brothers, but we are members of this country."

In declaring their villages "autonomous space" in the midst of the war, villagers "were reclaiming the right to life." These villagers attempted to create their own demilitarized zones in the slender swath of land that ran between the territory controlled by the paramilitaries and the FARC. A key clause in the agreements prohibited any armed group from entering their communities, either to kill or to recruit. The agreements also guaranteed there would be no collaboration with the army, guerrillas, or paramilitaries. This guarantee reflects a central concern of all communities that live in conflict zones. In a familiar pattern of terror and death, first the army enters a community and demands support, making the residents a guerrilla target. Conversely if the guerrillas enter the community, the civilians become targets of the paramilitaries and the army. Neutrality is afforded little respect in the bloody business of war.

And there was another demand that spoke of the desire for recognition—recognition as citizens and not "olvidados." The agreements included the demand for "moral reparation," in the form of monuments to the dead and "memory books" to list the names of those who had been killed, as well as to record the history of a people who remembered a time when they had lived "una vida sabrosa"—a delicious life.

Villagers were attempting to maintain their nonviolent struggle despite tremendous odds. One side of the river that flowed through their land was occupied by the paramilitaries. Standing on the left bank of the Atrato, one could look across the muddy water to the FARC territory that ran the length of the river's other bank. As the Atrato flowed through the thick jungle of Canyon Claro, enormous green leaves periodically gave way to burned-out homes that stood as testimony to the violence that had molded life for so many years. Yet, despite the helicopters overhead and the nearby thunder of machine-gun strafing, these villagers insisted on being more than "targets in a war we did not start." As one local leader insisted, "So far peace in Colombia has only existed in words or written documents. This is not enough. We must put peace into practice."

The challenges of practicing peace became apparent shortly after I arrived in Urabá with my two colleagues, Angela and Louise.[11] In our first meeting with María Cristina, she mentioned that the villagers in the Peace Community of Andalusia had requested accompaniment from the Catholic Church and the UN High Commissioner for Refugees to leave their land and join five other Peace Communities that had clustered together for security purposes in Costa de Oro. The Andalusians were living in the midst of combat and wanted safe passage downriver to the relative calm of Costa de Oro. They requested accompaniment, and an international presence would raise the political cost of lethal violence: one can kill anonymous peasants with alarming impunity.

Phone calls ensued, mosquito nets and knee-high rubber boots were purchased, and permission was secured for us to join the humanitarian commission that was charged with accompanying the villagers. María Cristina called us into her office to explain how delicate the situation was and to review the security measures the UN insisted we follow. "I want you to understand that the paramilitaries and the FARC are all over this area. You may be stopped and it is critically important that you do not speak. You might endanger everyone if you open your mouths. You might jeopardize the humanitarian space. The spokesperson for the group will be Miguel Ángel—he is the Defender of the People of Urabá. He and Vicente, from the government Social Solidarity Network, have years of experience with this sort of thing." Rounding out the commission were three outreach workers from the Catholic Church. Jaime,

María, and Wilson were all from the region and spent the bulk of each month living in the peace communities, providing material and moral support.

The next morning the UN truck picked us up at our hotel shortly before dawn. The forty-five-minute ride to the port at Turbo took us through banana plantations, rows planted as far as we could see. We heard the rumble of an airplane flying low overhead and realized we were up early enough to see the crop dusters that flew over the fields each day, clouds trailing in their wake. The director of the local health clinic had told us about these fumigations. He said cleft palates and miscarriages as well as chronic skin rashes were part of their patient profiles.

We arrived in Turbo a bit ahead of schedule and left the driver to watch the truck while we walked around. Ports do have that hey-sailor bustle about them. Stores were stocked with canned foods, appliances, clothes, compact discs, and shiny bicycles. There were easily a dozen large boats docked, and canoe-sized vessels were tied to poles all along the mouth of the gulf. A short time later the rest of the commission arrived, and we began loading the UN boat with the boxes of supplies the Social Solidarity Network was delivering, the food we had purchased to donate to the village, and our belongings. We slowly motored out of the harbor, stopping briefly at the military checkpoint. The soldiers reviewed the UN paperwork and we were waved on. The captain full-throttled our way across the gulf. The twin engines propelled us along the surface of the water and the ocean air laid salt crystals along our eyelashes and at the corners of our mouths.

The crossing was quick, and its completion was signaled by the sudden appearance of trees sticking up out of the water. We had arrived at the mouth of the Río Sucio—the "Dirty River." It was wide and easily navigable for those who had learned how to avoid the tree trunks. We tooled upriver, passing the towns of Riosucio and Domingodó. These towns were clusters of precarious wooden shacks on stilts, watermarks on weathered walls recording a history of recurrent flooding. A network of slender wooden planks was suspended on pilings several feet above the mud alleyways, and women walked single file down those planks to the river, enormous plastic baskets of laundry skillfully balanced on their heads.

Midafternoon found us at the small town of Curvaradó, a cluster of worn wooden shacks sprinkled along muddy roads. We spent the night because Jaime and María had some business to attend to, and the municipality maintained a large house with mattresses stacked up along the wall. The UN boat headed back to Turbo; from this point, the trip would be made in outdoor motorboats. The nuns prepared dinner and we finally fell asleep at three in the morning, when the corner store turned off its battery-powered disco beat.

It was three hours later when we began loading the five boats that would travel upriver to Andalusia. The motorists began coaxing their engines, gasoline fumes burning the hairs in our noses. We headed out, the boats obstinately facing the strong current that pulled against us all the way up to where Río Sucio merges into the Atrato River. An hour and a half later, Jaime pointed to a muddy clearing on the right bank of the river. "That's where we'll dock on the way back and walk to Costa de Oro." The village was not visible from the river—all we could see were palm trees and endless degrees of green.

Wilson suddenly called out to the boats behind us. Up ahead the river was blocked, piles of fallen trees and shrubs studiously placed across our path. As we approached the blockade, a volley of whistles passed from one side of the river to the other. The FARC controlled movement on the tributaries via blockades such as this one, which the motorists began hacking at with machetes. The slender branches were quickly cleared, but the large trunks below were easily a foot and a half in diameter. We carefully filed out of the boats, walking across the trunks and out of the way. Revving up their motors, the drivers raced the boats up and over the enormous trunks, belly flopping into the water on the other side. We tight-roped our way back out to the boats, and the whistling started up again.

Several bends later we passed Buena Vista, one of several deserted towns along the river. The paramilitaries had attacked Buena Vista several times before the villagers finally packed up everything they could carry on their backs and headed for the towns along the Atrato. We stopped for a few minutes to walk through the empty houses, school, and communal buildings. On the wall of the school, the letters AUC (Autodefensas Unidas de Colombia) had been drawn in white chalk.[12] Burned desks were tossed about in the corners, and several cows walked through on their way to graze. The school taught a gruesome lesson about the paramilitaries' growing power in the region and their determination to achieve territorial domination. We could hear machine-gun fire as we walked back to the boats.

When we finally pulled up close to the riverbank at Andalusia, the villagers were already waiting for us. We began passing our cargo to the human chain formed on the bank and joined the Andalusians in carrying everything through the mud up to the village. People offered us thick stalks of sugarcane that trickled sweet syrup down our faces as well as into our mouths. The villagers also carried up the two flags we had flown as we traveled upriver. A man laid the UN's and the diocese's flags out in the clearing in front of the communal kitchen, adding the Peace Communities sunshine flag to the display. Children pointed to the helicopters that were flying overhead—the flags were meant as proof of our presence and their neutrality.

At the request of Miguel Ángel and Vicente, the villagers convened a meeting. Under the thatch-roofed kitchen, we sat in a large circle and listened to the villagers explain the decision they had made. The meeting did not drown out the sound of machine-gun fire that echoed against the sides of the canyon. Several women shook their heads. "Listen to that. Our children can't sleep. Our heads hurt and our stomachs ache. We have to leave to save our lives."

An elderly couple began to speak. Emmadarda and her husband, Ramón, explained that the community had decided to leave Andalusia because the fighting had grown too near and too intense. Ramón shook his head. "I have worked this land all my life, but we have to leave. Maybe someday we can come back." His voice trailed off. People nodded silently, encouraging him to go on. It was Emmadarda who completed the thought. "We were getting ready to leave, but the FARC sent militia to tell us we have to stay. They told us we are not allowed to leave." Miguel Ángel interrupted. "Are you saying the FARC told you not to leave? Why weren't we told this before we left Apartadó?" He and Vicente became agitated, and the villagers sensed this.

Ramón explained: "We sent three emissaries to talk to the FARC and see if they could obtain permission for us to leave. We sent Rafael, Narciso, and Vladimiro. They left two days ago and still haven't come back. We want to wait until ten o'clock tomorrow morning, and if they aren't back by then, we need to leave." One of the women later explained to me that Vladimiro was just a teenager but had been chosen as an emissary because he was a bit mentally disabled and thus not likely to be detained and forcibly recruited. Both Rafael and Narciso were too old to be in danger of that.

Miguel Ángel suggested everyone sleep on it and reconvene at six o'clock the following morning. We were shown to a large open-air structure and began to hang up our mosquito nets. Miguel Ángel was positioned next to me on the wooden planks that would serve as our mattresses. "I feel impotent. The FARC have issued an order. An order is an order. I'm telling you, if I have to choose, I'm saving my own hide." He then tucked that hide into the net beside me and we all stretched out in a row and tried to sleep.

As the sounds of the bats in the thatched roof faded into our exhaustion, my friends nudged me. "Do you hear that?" I did. Several people were walking by the village, pausing to whisper, "They're over here." We did not move, holding still and letting the bat droppings bounce across the tops of our mosquito nets. It was an enormous relief when the walking began again and the FARC faded into the distance.

The morning meeting only served to reinforce the villagers' desire to leave. It took several hours for them to gather up their possessions. Bed frames, dressers, clothing, chickens, pots—everything we could hoist onto our backs was carried to the riverbank. The reality of only five motorboats sent the beds and dressers back up the muddy path. We packed peoples' belongings into every inch of those boats, piling children and other lightweight valuables on top. The boats sat low in the water, laden with many lifetimes. As we walked down the path from Andalusia to the waiting boats, Vicente kicked the dirt with his rubber boots: "All of this is about land. This whole damn war is about land."

One by one the young men on the bows of the boats pushed off from the bank with long wooden poles, turning the boats downriver. One poor skinny dog lunged into the water behind the boats. Her head bobbed in the current stirred up by the motors, her front legs furiously peddling in the water. She was so skinny it hurt to look at her. Someone finally took pity and dragged her into their boat by her front legs. We moved slowly under the weight. It was difficult to belly flop over tree trunks with such heavy loads. Each impasse was met with a flurry of machetes—these were new blockades that had been laid since the day before. The commission boat brought up the rear, flags flying off both sides.

About an hour downstream, we came around a bend to find the other four boats angled at a stop across the current. Our eyes followed the tilt of the heads raised toward a clearing in the palms. Three FARC militia stood on the riverbank, two with machine guns strapped over their shoulders, the third man with a radio in hand. He addressed the villagers angrily: "Shit, we told you not to leave. Shit. Get back up there right now or you'll pay the consequences!"

Wilson steered our boat up close to the bank and we waited for Miguel Ángel to speak. He was clearly terrified. "Good afternoon. Might we speak with your commander?" His request was denied as the guerrilla repeated their order: "The people back upriver, the institutions may continue." The villagers all looked toward our boat, waiting for Miguel Ángel to exercise his position as the Defender of the People. All went silent until he turned to Wilson and ordered him to head downriver. As the villagers thrust long poles into the silt on the river's bottom and slowly turned their boats around, the commission did not delay in heading downriver, the outboard motor spewing gasoline fumes and churning the water in its wake. It all happened so quickly that we were stunned. One lone voice asked, "But how are we going to leave all these people?" The only response was the drone of the motor.

We rode back in a silence as complete as the darkness that had fallen. Wilson knew the river so well that he wove between the floating trees without even a sliver of moon to guide him. When we docked at Curvaradó, everyone went to their separate corners of the municipality's large house. Later that night, we heard the floor creak and María's head peered around the doorway. She came in and sat on the edge of the mattress. She had already spoken with Jaime and Wilson, and they had decided they were going to head back upriver and bring the people down to Costa de Oro even if they had to rent a boat and go alone. María blended anger and concern: "We left those people with no food. There are two pregnant women and a young girl with malaria. But the worst thing is that they disobeyed the guerrillas and we left them there to go back all alone. We wondered if the three of you would consider going with us?"

* * *

The next morning, several children came running in to tell us a boat had just arrived. We looked out the doorway and saw two men walking toward us. They were two of the motorists who had accompanied us to Andalusia and who had stayed behind when their boats were detained. They were exhausted and hungry but alive. We sent money with one of the children and asked her to buy Coca-Cola and cookies while we embraced the two men and cried. They began telling us what had happened after they headed back upriver. The villagers had not gone all the way back up to Andalusia but had decided to dock at Villa Hermosa, about forty-five minutes from where the FARC had detained them. The motorists told us the villagers felt "muy engañados"—very tricked by what had happened. The state had failed them, and even the children talked about the fear they had seen in Miguel Ángel's eyes. They had passed the night listening to the machine-gun fire and wondering what the guerrillas would do.

They did not have to wait long to find out. That same evening, a group of militia arrived and called for a communal assembly. The comandante claimed his men had turned the villagers back for two reasons. They wanted to see what the state would do when challenged, and they expressed their amazement that no one in the commission had said a word. They also insisted they had stopped the villagers because the paras had established a base in the mouth of Canyon Claro, and the FARC were concerned the paras would open fire on the boats and slaughter everyone. Although this seemed a merely convenient version, subsequent events would indicate it was prescient.

Our capricious satellite phone kicked in and we patched our way through to the diocese and spoke with both Padre Leonides and his indispensable assistant, doña Pilar. They told us we could head upriver under the auspices of the diocese. They granted us permission to accompany the commission, thanking us for an international presence that would confer some security to all involved. Their permission and our borrowed satellite phone sealed the deal.

That evening we gathered and discussed the details. Father Honelio had arrived from the diocese and would speak on behalf of all of us. Father Honelio explained that in the event we were detained—by either the paramilitaries or the FARC—we would all stay together. Under no condition would we allow them to pull someone aside because we would not be likely to see them again. We would head to Villa Hermosa, where the villagers were waiting, and accompany them to Costa de Oro; those who chose to stay on for a few days were welcome to do so.

We set out in two boats the next day, meeting up with the other boats that were waiting with the villagers at Villa Hermosa. We were also joined by a wiry man named José Luis. He was one of the leaders of Costa de Oro and had come to Curvaradó to join us on the journey upriver. I think he wanted to make certain this commission had a different outcome. We followed the same route upriver, arriving at the sandy beach across from the mouth of Canyon Claro. Suddenly, the lull created by early morning air and the rocking of the boats was broken. "Get out of the boats now! Now, dammit. Fuck, get out of the boats now!" One by one, uniformed men began appearing from behind the palms. Each one pointed his machine gun to back up the command. Wilson and the other motorist steered us toward shore and we hurriedly got out of the boats. "Run! Run up the beach! Fuck! Now!" The machine guns waved us in the direction of the jungle and we ran as fast as we could through the porous sand. Father Honelio was in front of me; I reached out to touch his shoulder and let him know we had faith in him. In our rush, we did not tie up the boats, which began floating out with the current.

The jungle was so dense that we had to bend over as we ran, following a single track of worn mud. At regular intervals on each side of the path, a man with a machine gun told us to keep moving. I tried to discreetly peek out from under my baseball cap, and noticed crosses around many of their necks, reflecting the beams of sun that found their way through the leaves. First one, then five, then fifteen, then fifty-three paramilitaries appeared, each with a machine gun and rounds of ammunition wrapped around his chest. Some of the paras had mortar shells strapped to their thighs and others had radios in their hands. When we finally came to a stop, one young man radioed to his commander: "Eagle, we have the livestock right here. What do you want us to do with them?"

Another realization took place simultaneously. Once we stood up, it was clear that some of us were a gringa shade of white. Suddenly, the young "fuck-run-up-the-beach-now" para smiled. "Buenos días. How are you? Oh, don't be worried, we just want to talk to you." Another displayed his gift for rhetorical questions by asking us why we seemed nervous. Still another stared intensely: "Don't we know each other from somewhere?" At first this seemed an odd place to practice such a hackneyed pickup line. However, it may well be that he had seen us walking around Apartadó. Impunity was such that these young men moved between the jungle and the city with ease. Indeed, when we returned from Costa de Oro after the paras had stopped us, we looked at the young man staffing the military checkpoint. He smiled as he stared back at us, recognizing us from that day on the beach.

After a few minutes in which cigarettes were passed around our nervous circle, Eagle appeared, flanked by two heavily armed young men. Father Honelio began talking with him in low tones. He quietly looked the para in the eye and spoke calmly: "We are here on a humanitarian mission. Either we all stay or we all leave. We came together and will stay together." The para backed down, literally taking a step back into the palms behind him. More cigarettes were requested and puffed.

Eagle finally decided we could continue, satisfied with the explanation that we were only headed up Canyon Claro to help the villagers move to Costa de Oro. He told us we would be stopped again on the way down "to see what sort of people you have in those boats." We bent over and began the walk back to shore. At the end of the path, we were told to wait. Several paras opened fire, aiming at the other side of the river. The machine-gun fire was followed by several exploding mortar shells. As one of the men explained, "We want to make certain it is clear for you to walk to the boats." A more likely reason for firing was the hope that the FARC would fire back, killing us. Our blood would then be on someone else's hands. However, there was silence. We waded out to the boats and started up the motors. Looking back, all one could see was palm trees.

The trip upriver was long, the blockades many. When we finally reached Villa Hermosa, the villagers came running to the riverbank. The women were crying. Emmadarda and Ramón thanked us, insisting they knew we could come back for them. María had packed enormous bowls of food that we shared with the villagers; plates were passed and washed, and passed and washed again. The village president, Fernando, asked for everyone's attention. He explained the plan and the presence of the paras, assuring people that no one had to come along unless they wanted to. He added that it would be necessary to remain very calm—if anyone started to run away, the paras would shoot them in the back. Several men who had lost their documents opted to walk downriver. To be undocumented was to be suspect, and they were placing themselves in tremendous danger should they be detained. Father Honelio led us in prayer, asking that God protect us all on the way to Costa de Oro. We loaded the boats and slowly wound our way downriver.

It was a different group of FARC militia that detained us this time, ordering Father Honelio to go with them. The wait wore on and the rain began to fall. The motorists jumped onto shore and used their machetes to cut down a pile of enormous leaves. We passed them around in the boats, using them as umbrellas as the rain pounded down. Two hours later Father Honelio and three militia came back down and told us we had permission to continue on to Costa de Oro. We waved our leaves to celebrate and everyone started to cheer. The high spirits continued until shortly before the mouth of the river. Everyone had been told the paras would be waiting; I could hear people gasp as men began to appear from behind the trees. The motorists pulled up as close to the shore as they could and we began to file out of the boats. Several more men appeared to search the boats, while the rest of us were herded over to one side of the shore. There were fifteen heavily armed men standing before us. I had pulled two of the children near to me. They were trembling, and little Javier was embarrassed when a stream of pee ran down his pant leg and puddled into the sand.

One of the paras asked people what they thought they were doing. Ramón stepped to the front and told him, "We don't owe you anything. This is our land and we just want to work." He was abruptly cut off by one of the paras, who scoffed, "All this land belongs to the guerrillas and we are going to finish them all off." While this man continued to harass Ramón, another para asked the villagers how his aunt was. Everyone from Andalusia knew him—he used to be one of the FARC commanders in the area and he had family in Villa Hermosa. He then radioed Eagle: "Do you want me to separate out the ones

I know?" We could hear both outgoing and incoming calls. "Who are they with?" He replied that they were with a humanitarian commission. The channel crackled, "Then tell them to have a good trip in the name of the Autodefensas Unidas de Colombia." We were allowed back into the boats and continued on to Costa de Oro.

We could see the outline of human forms on the riverbank, and loud whoops let out when the boats approached the shore. The villagers at Costa de Oro had heard the shots that had been fired several hours earlier and had no idea if we had all been killed. As we unloaded the boats and headed up the path, Yulie, one of the girls from Andalusia, began to explain to Jaime that the men who had stopped us were really soldiers and not paramilitaries. We knew they were indeed paras but were interested in why she was convinced they were not. As she explained, "I know they were soldiers because if they'd been paras they would have killed every single one of us. That's what paras always do."

* * *

In response to the villagers' request, we remained with them for a month in Costa de Oro. We were told that an international presence in their communities kept the armed groups at bay. The weeks that followed provided many opportunities for conversations that lasted late into the hot, sticky nights. People reminisced about how life used to be: when they could tend their crops, celebrate their fiestas, and watch their children grow, trusting they would have a future to grow into. They spoke repeatedly of the "delicious life" they had enjoyed before the fighting engulfed them, contrasting that past with a present "that tastes like food without salt."

A "life without salt" underscored the role of war in the production of poverty. Before the fighting escalated dramatically in the mid-1990s, these villagers cultivated bananas and sold them to the merchants who ran the twelve to fifteen boats that had regularly traveled up and down the Atrato River. A family could earn one hundred dollars a week selling bananas, a source of income that was cut off with the economic blockade imposed by the paras. The paramilitaries had set a limit on how much merchandise villagers were allowed to transport upriver. The round trip from Costa de Oro to the stores in Riosucio cost approximately twenty-five dollars, and the paras prohibited the transport of more than fifteen dollars in goods on the grounds that anything in excess of that amount must be going to provision the FARC. The FARC, in turn, constructed the ever-changing physical blockades that required machetes and chain saws to clear. Traveling the river was expensive and dangerous.

The inability to travel freely on the river had other consequences as well. Many state agencies and nongovernmental organizations were unable to find people who were willing to travel upriver. That meant the teachers no longer arrived, the health post had no medicine, and the sick had limited options. Those limited options could be fatal.

A few days after we arrived, I noticed the health promoter, Carmen, fanning something on the floor of her front porch. A closer look revealed it was someone and not something. A baby lay on a bed of cool green leaves designed to lower a fever that had been raging for forty-eight hours. Her tiny chest raised and lowered in jerking spurts, large swollen lumps beneath her skin pressing the life out of her tiny body. I searched my backpack but only had ibuprofen, and that little person clearly needed something stronger than that. Carmen held up a bottle of pink baby antibiotic, the contents dry and cracking against the sides of the vial. The nearest health post was in Riosucio, that expensive and dangerous destination downriver. The parents were too afraid to risk the trip, and the community could not spare able-bodied men for such a dangerous venture. When word spread throughout Costa de Oro that the baby had died, people insisted her death was not Carmen's fault. No, people were adamant in their reckoning: "That baby was a casualty of war."

Aftermaths

How does war move through the tissue, blood, and bone of combatants and noncombatants, and through the living body of the land and rivers as well? The ebb and flow of the Atrato offers some answers. The baby would not appear on any official body count, of course. Even if she did figure into a graph somewhere, her cause of death would most likely be "high fever" or "failure to thrive." Those categories reference the proximate cause, erasing the belligerent context in which her parents and community had exercised the painful ethics of triage.

And what of Javier and Yulie? They survived Costa de Oro, but can anyone believe they came through unscathed? Patrick Clarkin reminds his readers that, "depending on local circumstances, a developing embryo, infant, or child growing up embroiled in armed conflict is likely to face—directly or indirectly—various stressors, including malnutrition, infectious diseases and/or psychological stress."[13] The impact of these stressors may not manifest for years, perhaps erasing the tracks of their etiology. I do not suggest these children are doomed to join the ranks of the walking wounded, but certainly the long reach of war requires time depth and a combination of epigenetic and ethnographic research. This combination can explore how war has left its mark, without falling into "somatic determinism" and hopelessness.[14] Ethnographic research can assist *and* insist on foregrounding the multiple environments in which reproduction unfolds.[15]

And what of that yearning, that longing for *una vida sabrosa*—a delicious life? It is more than salt the adults miss. When Ramón shook his head and lamented, "I have worked this land all of my life, but we have to leave"; when folks were displaced and spent years "wandering in foreign land"; when still others insisted, "The river is identity and memory. The river is its people and its people are the river": How can we begin to grasp the pain of being dislodged from ecosystems that have been part of kinship networks, or grasp mourning a way of life that has been violently taken away?[16] Before the toxic chemicals from the mining industry met up with deforestation, before the aerial pesticides clinging to the banana trees magnified the slow leeching of land mines into the soil, the Río Atrato was known for its abundance. Adults insist it did not matter where you came from or who you were; alongside the river you had sustenance. "If you stayed an entire month, you had a month to eat without spending a cent. The river would sustain you." In fact, one nickname for the river was "criaguachos"—someone or something that raises the orphans.[17] The river itself was part of a circle of care in an interdependent world, with that interdependence understood as a condition, one that made possible river lifeways.[18] Now the land was poisoned, the river polluted, the fish depleted. Nostalgia is not a strong enough word to describe this.

I am persuaded by the work of Ashlee Cunsolo and Neville Ellis, which is based upon their sustained research in Canada and Australia. Listening carefully to their interlocutors talk about climate change–related loss led them to consider "ecological grief." As they define it, this is "the grief felt in relation to experienced or anticipated ecological losses, including the loss of species, ecosystems and meaningful landscapes due to acute or chronic environmental change."[19] Although ecological grief has yet to figure into most discussions of climate change or environmental research, perhaps that reflects the privileged position of those who study planetary change from the position of an outsider rather than a party to the devastation.

For now, back to the belligerent environment, the land and water upon and against which war was waged. Bombs exploding, trees felled, mass graves, land mines sown across the country, exploded gas pipelines seeping into rivers, aerial fumigation: these are the more-than-human wages of war.[20] How does one measure and respond to the environmental degradation inflicted by armed conflict?[21] Once again, Colombia is setting a precedent.

Wounded Warscapes

Why do people separate nature from the human? The conception of ethnic peoples is that the territory is inseparable from the people. We want to strengthen a line of thought that allows us to understand that all living beings, not just human beings, have the possibility of existing.

—BELKIS IZQUIERDO, judge, Special Jurisdiction for Peace, Colombia (quoted in Calle, "La JEP reconoce que la naturaleza es víctima del conflict")

On the two-lane highway that runs between Apartadó and Turbo, Evangelical churches vie for space between motels that rent by the hour, car repair shops, open-air markets, banana fields, and innumerable small family stores.[22] Their proprietors hose down dusty plastic chairs at dawn, then set them out front to entice passersby seeking some shade while waiting for the next bus or perhaps some small talk over a cold bottle of soda.

I had jumped off the bus a few minutes outside Apartadó and tried to get my bearings. I was looking for the home of a pastor who had once been a fearsome paramilitary. As vocation would have it, he was out preaching. The walk back to the main road was a sweaty one, and a plastic chair in the shade was enticing. I shooed a few scraggly chickens away and eagerly bit off the corner of a flimsy plastic bag of water.

The owner was an older woman who had lived in that small wooden house for many years. Yamila lived alone, and I became a regular customer. She enjoyed telling me stories, although she would always stop if anyone else was within hearing range. She had survived some of the most violent years in the region, violence that had displaced many peasants who ran for their lives. One afternoon she gestured toward the hills and told me about the Curva de Diablo (Devil's Curve). It lay at the crest of the hill, on a dirt path that was used to transport goods inland as well as to flee when the paramilitaries arrived with chainsaws. Once the paras realized people were attempting to escape, they positioned a few armed men at the Curva de Diablo with orders to kill anyone they encountered and to dump the bodies beside the road. Those bodies accumulated and loved ones were not allowed to bury the dead. Blood seeped deep into the soil. "Even now," Yamila added, "that place is not right. People try to take their goods inland, they pack up their horses. But the horses stop and tremble when they reach the Curva de Diablo. They refuse to pass through—their owners have to whip them. The horses are terrified. It's because the land remembers."

Recall that on June 10, 2011, former president Juan Manuel Santos signed into law the Ley de Víctimas y Restitución de Tierras, Law 1448 (Victims and Land Restitution Law). This law was explicitly focused on victims and their right to a range of reparations.[23] Consistent with the UN's Basic Principles and Guidelines on the Right to a Remedy and Reparation for Victims of Gross Violations of International Human Rights Law and Serious Violations of International Humanitarian Law, the Victims Law called for "comprehensive reparations," including restitution, compensation, rehabilitation, satisfaction, and guarantees of nonrepetition. The Colombian government presented this law as a mechanism that would facilitate the restitution of millions of hectares of lands abandoned or stolen as a result of human rights abuses and violations. While scant land has been returned to its owners, Law 1448 did acknowledge the existence of an armed conflict, something that the government of Álvaro Uribe had refused to do.

Important components of Law 1448 are Decrees 4633 and 4635, which detail the rights of Indigenous and Afro-Colombian communities and territories.[24] As Article 3 of Decree 4633 states: "For indigenous peoples, the territory is a victim, taking into account their worldview and the special and collective bond that unites them with Mother Earth."[25] This is further elaborated in Article 45, which acknowledges, "The territory, understood as a living integrity and sustenance of identity and harmony, according to the worldview of indigenous peoples and by virtue of the special and collective bond that they maintain with it, suffers damage when it is violated or desecrated by the internal armed conflict and its related and underlying factors."[26] Decree 4635 echoes this "special relationship" with regard to Afro-Colombian communities: "The survival of the communities implies the effective exercise of their collective right over their territories, by virtue of the close cultural relationship that they maintain with them. The territory is recognized and understood as the fundamental basis of its cultures, its spiritual life, its integrity and its autonomous development."[27] Taken together, these various articles provide the legal scaffolding for a new vision of what constitutes a casualty of war and have allowed both the Colombian Constitutional Court and the Special Jurisdiction for Peace to make a series of important rulings.

In 2016, the Constitutional Court officially announced ruling T-622: the Atrato River, that same winding river that members of the Peace Communities had sailed as they sought refuge in Costa de Oro, was "deserving of rights as guaranteed by the Constitution."[28] According to the Court, "nature is a true subject of rights that must be recognized by states and exercised . . . for the communities that inhabit it or have a special relationship with it."[29] The land rights organization Tierra Digna underscored the importance of this ruling, noting it was the first time the Constitutional Court had worked within the new framework of "biocultural rights" to recognize the Atrato River as "a living entity that sustains other forms of life and cultures."[30] Among the factors enumerated as having contributed to the degradation of the Atrato, gold mining and the armed conflict warranted special mention.

There is synergy between this ruling and the work of the Jurisdicción Especial para la Paz (JEP, Special Jurisdiction for Peace). One component of Colombia's 2016 Peace Accords between the government and the FARC included provisions for a Sistema Integral de Verdad, Justicia, Reparación y No Repetición (SIVJRNR, Comprehensive System of Truth, Justice, Reparation and Non-repetition). The system is composed of the Truth, Coexistence and Non-repetition Commission, frequently referred to as the Truth Commission; the Unit for the Search for Persons Presumed Disappeared in the context and by reason of the armed conflict; comprehensive reparation measures for peace building and guarantees of non-repetition; and the Special Jurisdiction for Peace.[31]

The JEP was designed to uncover and adjudicate serious human rights violations that were committed during the country's internal armed conflict. These crimes include kidnapping, torture, extrajudicial executions, sexual violence, forced displacement, and the recruitment of minors. Blending retributive and restorative justice, one intent of the JEP is to encourage the accused to offer full confessions of their crimes and assume responsibility for their actions in exchange for reduced sentences. If the accused admit to their crimes up front, they may receive an alternative sentence that deprives them of various personal liberties, with sentences ranging from five to eight years for serious crimes and two to five years for lesser offenses. Alternative sentences can include a combination of house arrest and community service, to be meted out in agreement with the victims to whom the accused may owe reparations. Among the reparation measures considered by the JEP are the removal of land mines and explosives from territories in which the FARC had operated; finding, identifying, and returning the remains of people who were disappeared during the conflict; new judicial mechanisms to dismantle criminal organizations; and the restitution of land titles.

The above is a familiar and important list of transitional justice measures. Colombia's innovation lies in moving beyond an anthropocentric framework of human rights to recognize the environment itself as a victim of the armed conflict. Building upon Law 1448 and its decrees, the JEP has incorporated the "principles, logics and rationalities of ethnic peoples' justice systems, with the aim of seeking truth through conscience, reconciliation healing and the harmonization between victims and the accused that will allow for strengthening the communal fabric, as well as promote harmonization with the territory."[32] Territory is more than land: it is a living entity with agency, a vital player and not merely a backdrop to human life.[33]

I recall Vicente kicking the dirt with his foot as we left Andalusia. "All of this is about land. This whole damn war is about land." I agree that the decades of armed conflict in Colombia were in part a resource war, and control of land has been (and remains) a key source of contention. In fact, the concentration of land in the hands of drug traffickers and cattle ranchers resulted in a "counteragrarian reform" that pushed hundreds of thousands of peasant farmers off their land.[34] This was also an oil war. Oil, as a fixed asset, contributes to the struggle over land: the only way to access the oil is to control the land from which it is to be pumped. Oil literally fueled the conflict. But land as a resource fails to capture a "vernacular landscape" peopled with sacred sites, medicinal plants, rivers, mountains, and animal kin. As Rob Nixon defines it, "A vernacular landscape is shaped by the affective, historically textured maps that communities have devised over generations, maps replete with names and routes, maps alive to significant ecological and surface geological features. A vernacular landscape, although neither monolithic nor undisputed, is integral to the socioenvironmental dynamics of community rather than being wholly externalized—treated as out there, as a separate nonrenewable resource."[35] The blood and memories that seeped into the soil at Curva de Diablo call out for reckoning, which in turn might allow the souls of the dead and of the land to find some peace.

* * *

Such reckoning may be possible in Colombia. The JEP has the authority to select and prioritize the cases that fall under its jurisdiction. As of January 2020, the JEP had opened seven cases—collectively referred to as the Macro-Cases—which encompass different crimes categorized either by the zone of occurrence or by the type of crime. One such case is Case 002, "The Territorial Situation of the Municipalities of Tumaco, Ricaurte and Barbacoas (Nariño)." The JEP conducted a two-year investigation of crimes and harms inflicted between

January 1, 1990, and December 1, 2016, by the FARC and the Public Forces (Armed Forces and National Police) upon Indigenous and Afro-Colombian communities. The JEP investigated crimes such as internal displacement, assassinations, sexual violence, torture, and forced recruitment—and focused on the "socio-environmental and territorial" harms that Afro-Colombian Consejos Comunitarios (Community Councils) and Awá and Eperara Siapiadaara Reservations suffered in the region.

Here I highlight three decisions and what they mean for communities, territories—and for "distributed reproduction." Decision 074 of 2018 and Decisions 032 and 079 of 2019 collectively refer to the impact of the armed conflict on the environment, underscoring the hazardous effects of activities such as deforestation, illegal mining, illegal crops (particularly coca crops, which are tied in with toxic fumigation), and attacks on oil pipelines, a combination of which were used by different combatants to finance the conflict in the region.[36]

With Decision 079, the JEP refers to the centrality of Katsa Su for the Awá Indigenous people. For the Awá, Katsa Su is the world as a whole, including the territory, people, and all species. In its ruling, the JEP's Chamber for the Recognition of Truth, Responsibility and the Determination of Facts and Conducts stated:

> According to the Awá people, they belong to the "Katsa Su," which is alive, is mother earth, the fountain of good living and the house of the Awá people and the beings that inhabit it. In the Katsa Su the Awá people carry out every experience of spirituality. . . . Effectively, for the indigenous peoples as the Great Awá Family, the world is not dual, everything is one, interrelated and interdependent; there is no separation between the material, the cultural and the spiritual. Also, everything is alive and sacred, not just human beings, but also hills, caves, water, houses, plants, and animals have social agency. . . . Then, the Katsa Su is woven from relationships endowed of sacred significance and integrated by diverse communal, social, and natural relations underlying the existence and identity of the Awá People. In words of a member of the Awá People: "without territory, we do not exist."[37]

This was the first time, within transitional justice, that a sacred stone, a stream of water, our kin that fly, or a verdant swath of forest were judged to be victims of war rather than a mere backdrop or collateral damage. It is a start.

* * *

A rapid inventory is in order: children born of rape, wombs and uterine myopia, blaming mothers no matter what they do, toxic environments, epigenetics and situated biologies, war and its legacies. I wish now to bring these made-to-seem-disconnected realms into dialogue across time and space. How are things made to seem disparate and who are the "bewilderers" who might benefit from conjuring distraction?[38]

Through Law 1448 and its decrees, as well as through the JEP's rulings, the broader public is reminded of the "special relationship," "the special and collective bond" that Indigenous and Afro-Colombian communities have with the land. I do not question this at all; this is equally true of Quechua-speaking communities in Peru. But what is the history of severing that "special relationship" such that "discovering" it can seem innovative? By bracketing Indigenous and Afro-Colombian communities and *their* special relationships, what disconnect is reinstantiated for everyone else?

In Colombia, "los territorios" seems to refer to everywhere that is *not* Bogotá. "Los territorios" stamp both a region and its inhabitants as "other," a move that is also enshrined in the widely applied "enfoque diferencial" (differential focus). The term appears in the Peace Accords and Law 1448, and it is omnipresent on state and NGO websites.[39] What is it and to whom does it apply? *Enfoque diferencial* is an identity-based approach to program design and delivery, and it seems to apply to anyone who is not a light-skinned, heterosexual, able-bodied middle- or upper-class urban male. It is women, sexual minorities, Indigenous populations, children, the elderly, and the disabled, among others. It is admittedly well intentioned and informed by the politics of recognition and its "logic of enumeration," by which political and theoretical efficacy presumably exist only through naming each category of selfhood or experience.[40] The problem is that it leaves certain people (light-skinned, heterosexual, able-bodied middle- or upper-class urban males) as the generic category of the "human" against which others are marked and somehow deviate. This generic human does not, presumably, have a special relationship with the land or with the forest, rivers, stones, or other living creatures that share this world. The severing of that relationship, however, has a *particular* history, tethered inescapably to settler colonialism, rapacious capitalism, and plunder. With its "enfoque diferencial"—of which the "enfoque territorial" is one component—the Colombian transitional justice process is limited in terms of its transformative potential. Indigenous and Afro-Colombian communities are no match for the legacies of the armed conflict *and* the proliferation of extractive industries as long as other sectors of the population do not see themselves as having a shared future at stake, one that is entangled with our more-than-human kin.

"Without territory we do not exist." The statement underscores that reproduction, social and otherwise, occurs within *and* beyond the womb. Martine Lappé, Robin Jeffries Hein, and Hannah Landecker have traced the emergence of an environmental reproductive justice framework, attuned to the structural forces that shape reproductive outcomes.[41] The insistence on the political ecology of reproductive labor can help move policy debates beyond individualized narratives of responsibility, which place the burden on women to enact "good motherhood" regardless of the circumstances of conception or the toxic environment in which they dwell.[42] This expanded definition of the "maternal environment" could lead to theoretical insights and contribute to an explicitly feminist environmental agenda with an incisive intersectional component.[43]

For example, what about men? Fathers? As Sarah Richardson reminds us, "Males provide parental care in many species, and male gametes are also subject to environmental exposures that may affect future generations."[44] In spite of the paternal contribution to maternal and child environments, in the exponentially plural, there is scant research on paternal effects. This would seem odd given the centrality of patriarchal biology in many theories of transmission; however, it is the potentially/actually reproducing female that is clearly the primary target of prenatal and perinatal interventions. Taking a distributed approach to reproduction could allow for greater attention to biological and social fathers; to communities that embrace or reject children born of wartime rape; to injurious names that may mark a child in lasting ways; to account for postwar landscapes steeped in toxins. In sum, this approach could help ensure that the insights of epigenetics and situated biologies do not lead to even greater efforts to govern maternal bodies.[45]

These two Colombian precedents—reparations for children born of wartime rape and recognition that the environment is a victim of armed conflict—could provide an important way forward if the two constructively converge. When members of the Standing Rock Sioux Reservation began protesting the proposed Dakota Access pipeline, one phrase captured the possibilities inherent in such a convergence: "Environmental Justice Is Reproductive Justice."[46] Implicit in this claim is the recognition that reproduction occurs in multiple, diverse, yet entwined bodies. With this in mind, I suggest we ask the following: What is reproductive violence and where does it occur? Where do we look for it, and how do we attempt to provide remedy? In no way do I wish to minimize the violence done to individual bodies; rather, I wish to grasp the relationships that have been severed and to call out for care and repair. An example from the highlands of Peru conveys this well.

Epidemic: Witches, Gods, and Bones

A key figure in diagnosing witchcraft and settling accounts in the community of Carhuahurán was don Teofilo, the *curandero* (healer).[47] Teofilo was a tiny man—indeed, his nickname was El Piki (Quechua for "flea"). Teofilo was called upon to read the coca leaves and bodily symptoms; to name a perpetrator when witchcraft is determined; and to head out to the mountains and speak with the *apus*—the mountain gods who were angry that the villagers forgot them during the years of war, causing the gods to ally with the enemy.

Teofilo was wary of me when I first arrived, wondering what this gringa was going to do with all she hoped to learn. During one of our initial conversations, Teofilo issued a thinly veiled challenge: "So you want to know what I do? The words I use are so powerful that I could destroy you just by speaking them. Do you want me to speak them right now? Do you really think you have the power to handle my words?" He began to laugh, clearly pleased by my discomfiture. I felt very small indeed. He was, after all, the man who knew the language that allowed him to climb the sharp peaks surrounding Carhuahurán and converse with the mountain gods, soliciting advice and appeasing their anger.

Several months after don Teofilo had put me in my place, he did begin to share a bit of his knowledge, although I was never fully trusted by this powerful, tiny man. He assured me there was an epidemic throughout the highlands: there was *daño* (witchcraft); *alcanzo*, an illness caused by the *apus* (mountain gods) who punish the person who sits or steps where they should not; and *aya*, caused by coming into contact with the bones of the gentiles (ancestors). The gentiles were the people who lived before the time of Christ, and God sent down a rain of fire to punish them for being envious. They attempted to save themselves by entering the mountains, where their remains continue to cause illness to the unfortunate people whose bones they invade.

These illnesses began to increase uncontrollably in 1984 when the fighting became so intense that both life and the landscape were in upheaval. People began fleeing, sleeping in caves for fear of attacks. As El Piki explained, "In those times we escaped to the mountains, we slept in the caves. That's why we're sick. We're always getting sick. *Alcanzo* grabbed us—*aya* grabbed us. We were sleeping in caves with the bones of the gentiles. That's why so many people died with weakness. It's a slow wasting, until you die because the illness matures inside you."

Once military bases were established throughout the countryside, campesinos were obligated to live in nucleated settlements for security purposes. This new spatial practice gave rise to more *envidia* (envy) as neighbors now lived next door as opposed to a steep slope away. Witchcraft accusations soared, and people were dying. The fighting also made it too dangerous for El Piki to head out regularly to the mountains and place *pagapus* (offerings or sacrifices) on behalf of villagers who were requesting godly intervention in resolving problems: "I could no longer speak regularly with Madre Rasuhuillca [Mother Rasuhuillca, the highest mountain in the region]. She is *la señora de la medicina, la señora abogada* [the lady of medicine, the lady lawyer]."

In a time of profoundly conflictive social relationships—envious neighbors as well as different alliances during the war, which generated tremendous distrust—Madre Rasuhuillca grew angry that villagers had forgotten their commitments to her. She sided with the enemy, allowing them to hide in the clouds surrounding her peak, the shrubs clustered on her slopes, and the holes in the earth that she opened for the guerrillas when they were pursued by the armed peasant patrols. As numerous patrollers recalled, "When we went out to Rasuhuillca on patrol, we found flowers, cigarettes, limes— the guerrillas took *pagapus*. They had a pact with the mountains and that was why they could hide in the hills. The mountains opened up to let them in, and then hid them."

Virtually every villager was suffering from *alcanzo* or had recently recovered. Don Teofilo was called upon on a daily basis to climb up to the *puna* and try to repair villagers' relationships with the gods as well as cure them of the witchcraft performed by all-too-human perpetrators. El Piki treated social strife and conflictive relations. Madre Rasuhuillca was both doctor and lawyer; healing the individual body meant reconciling in the social sphere—a sphere shared with bones of the ancestors, rivers that ran red with blood, and mountains that held a lethal grudge.

Reproductive politics and environmental politics do indeed share a "special connection," one that should not be bracketed as true only for Others. That bracketing is one pillar of human exceptionalism; another pillar is the bounded, atomized, masculine individual who enters unencumbered into the social contract after rationally weighing the costs and benefits of doing so. Time to think anew—no one I know ever liked that guy much anyway.

One critique of transitional justice is its foundation in a narrow liberal rights tradition, limiting its capacity to effect structural change.[48] The Colombian Peace Accords are, to my mind, a largely neoliberal package with glimmers of transformative potential. A considerable portion of that potential lies in naming and denouncing reproductive violence writ large, across multiple environments and bodies. There is a vital connection between the questions researchers ask and the responsibilities their answers produce. Donna Haraway has issued an invitation: "It is high time that feminists exercise leadership in imagination, theory, and action to unravel ties of both genealogy and kin, and kin and species."[49] Indigenous epistemologies offer important insights for anyone wishing to send an affirmative RSVP.

4

THE LONG WAY AROUND

I begin my Gender Theory and Praxis course with a thought experiment on gender:

A Thought Experiment

What does gender have to do with

- A mountain?
- Drinking water?
- A steep path?
- The long way forward?

As it turns out, gender has a great deal to do with it.

In 1995, communities throughout Ayacucho, Peru, were left in ruins: burned houses, abandoned farmlands, and innumerable mass graves converted the earth itself into yet another actor in this tragedy. The social landscape was equally volatile as campesinos struggled to rebuild their communities in the shadow of a recent past marked by lethal, intimate violence. The memories were palpably fresh, painful, omnipresent. "Rumi Llaqta" was no exception.

As happened in many communities, the all-male authorities had petitioned for the installation of a military base for "protection." The soldiers occupied the base for more than a decade during the internal armed conflict. It sat high on a hill, a panopticon that brought daily life under its controlling gaze. Communal agreements implied certain sexual agreements: the men in these communities built the bases that multiplied throughout Ayacucho during the violence, while women and girls "serviced" the troops. In some communities, sex became commodified as women began selling sex. Far more common, however, was rape. Members of the surrounding communities concurred: in Rumi Llaqta, the soldiers had committed massive rape, "hasta las niñas" (even the girls).

The base sat slightly beyond the scope of the photo included here, high on the hill in the upper righthand corner.[1] By the time I arrived, the soldiers came through on a rotating basis, staying for several weeks or months at a time, depending on the level of perceived threat. The community was classified as bordering a "zona roja" (red zone), implying the guerrillas still maintained a presence, or at least some sympathy, in the area.

There was a highland lake just on the other side of the steepest slope, and long black tubing ran the length of the mountain, all the way down to a water spigot located in the middle of the village. Each morning and evening, women and children (and the occasional widower with no family to care for him) headed to the spigot and waited to fill brightly colored plastic buckets and pitchers with water. There was no waiting in impatient silence. This was a social gathering and gossip central, offering a chance to find out which schoolteacher was sleeping with the engineer, whose goat had eaten the neighbor's fava beans, and whether or not they would *ever* finish the highway.

At that point all able-bodied men were required to participate in the nocturnal peasant patrol, shots in the middle of the night indicating it was time for the next rotation. It was bitterly cold and the stone watchtowers were no match for the wind. Daybreak was time for agricultural labors, a seemingly interminable effort to cultivate fields that had laid fallow during the armed conflict. The men were understandably exhausted.

"Rumi Llaqta," 1997

As (bad) luck would have it, the tubing broke. The damage was such that entire sections needed to be replaced. A communal assembly was convened to determine what to do. Communal assemblies were obligatory for all adult men and the widows, the latter being considered heads of household. Buying more tubes would entail levying a contribution on each household, sending several men and pack animals down to the city of Huanta, spending at least one night in a hotel, eating meals in the city, and then coming back up with the heavy supplies required to repair that long black line. A vote was taken and the idea was nixed. It was, after all, women and children who fetched water.

Without the tubing, going for water became something of an alpine expedition. Buckets and pitchers in hand, we headed up the hill to the lake, those heavy containers pulling on our arms as we balanced our way back down. It was about ten to fifteen minutes up and another ten to fifteen minutes back down. Twice a day. Then the soldiers returned to the base, the base that sat adjacent to the path laid bare when the tubing broke.

The women and children continued to make the trek, but there were rumors and concerns. The mothers told their daughters not to look at or smile at the soldiers: "Just stare at your feet like we do." But the rumors did not subside, and bored soldiers made for wolf whistles . . . and more. Rumors flamed into outright fear and led to the search for another path.

As it turned out, there was a roundabout way of heading up those steep slopes. You could walk up the ridge visible on the far left of the photo, then circle back along the crest to the lake. That path did not pass by the base; that long way around took twenty to thirty minutes up and another twenty to thirty minutes down. Twice a day. The boys still took the other route because the soldiers expressed no interest in them. Sixty minutes stretched into 120, at least for the women and girls.

The fields were still yielding primarily potatoes, which was virtually the only food on hand. We ate potatoes as soup for breakfast and boiled potatoes with salt as snacks, and potato soup again at the end of the day. At one point, the truck up from Huanta arrived laden with large tin cans of USAID cooking oil. The excitement was palpable: deep fried potatoes. The variety was well received. Food was scarce and protein even more so. When times are tough and food is hard to find, who is fed first?

At this point in class, the hands shoot up. "Babies!" "Little kids!" I feel a bit guilty at times, knowing I will disappoint the optimists. People were hungry; able-bodied men were in short supply. Who was fed first? Men. Then male adolescents. Then elderly men if they had family members. Then little boys, then the women. Then the girls. Babies came last, but before the scrawny dogs. I recall the fortified milk they distributed at the health post: Did they ever trace where it ended up? People insisted the powdered milk gave the babies diarrhea, which may have been true. All I know is that the powdered milk usually ended up in the big black pot of potato soup boiling over the family fire.

The gendered dimensions of mountains, drinking water, and steep paths: it was women and little girls—precisely those children most likely to be poorly fed with empty bellies rumbling—who took the calorically demanding long way around.

Vocabularies of Violation: Toward a Gendered
Theory of Harm

In the aftermath of armed conflicts, one task of transitional justice processes is investigating human rights violations and proposing appropriate forms of remedy.[2] In her updated text on truth commissions, Priscilla Hayner notes that it is only within the last two decades that there has been a significant expansion in the literature on reparations.[3] Increasingly, reparations programs figure as a staple ingredient of transitional justice endeavors due to the realization that satisfying demands for justice requires more than doing something *to* the perpetrators; it means doing something *for* the victim-survivors as well.

Reparations programs and other forms of redress operate on the maxim "where there is a right, there is a remedy." This is part of the problem: the classic violations enshrined in human rights treaties default to masculinist normativity and legal categories that fail to capture what many women prioritize as the most harmful consequences of war. This reflects the limitations of the liberal legal realm, which is characterized by an "accountability approach" in which the daily violence women experience has yet to be legally defined. If it is a right that must be violated in order to trigger the remedy, then many forms of gendered harm will be rendered illegible. Although strides have been made in terms of sexual violence, there are many other ways in which girls and women experience war. There is forced labor, coerced marriage, forced sterilization, displacement, male-biased land tenure system and inheritance patterns, chronic health problems stemming from sexual violence and malnutrition, forced motherhood, and the sharp rise in female-headed households and the feminization of poverty. These gender-based harms are overwhelmingly born by women and girls: prosecuting sexual crimes alone will not achieve the transformative structural changes that are required at the international and domestic levels. As my colleague Dyan Mazurana notes, "In war more men are killed, but more women die."[4] The "slower dying" may fall outside the temporal and legal categories that are grounded in the violation of male bodies.

Feminist legal theorists have provided compelling critiques of law and liberalism, underscoring the failure of both to adequately capture the experiences of women. Fionnuala Ní Aoláin has referred to this as the "problem of capture."[5] As she argues, "The idea of harm to women has been central to women's placement in legal discourse. Such placement however is not synonymous with status and recognition."[6] Indeed, the conceptual and practical consequences of such efforts frequently affirm women's secondary and disjunctive social status and give rise to regulatory or protectionist legal regimes that may be constraining and paternalist in their application.

One can examine international law regulations that seek to "protect" women via the laws of armed conflict and human rights and yet remain silent on reproductive rights, specifically abortion. The protective impulse here is a child- and fetus-oriented one such that "woman and children" appear as a barely hyphenated unit, resulting in a legal scaffolding that cannot conceptually conceive of the inherent tension in the relationship. For example, in a sympathetic text on children born of war, Joanne Neenan argues that "any normative or policy construction of false binaries between 'women's rights' (for mothers only) versus 'children's rights' (for children born of sexual violence) misses the ongoing impact of gender discrimination on children born of sexual violence and obscures the fact that many mothers are also still children."[7] I disagree. These are, at times, competing rights regimes that cannot be willed away, and to reject this as a false binary fails to consider that these fetuses and babies may be experienced as a form of harm to the women who birth them. When we consider the vocabulary that women use to describe the violence done to themselves and others, recall the names given to some of the children by their own mothers.

In her thoughtful analysis of gender-based and sexual violence during the Holocaust, Ní Aoláin revisits what is too frequently presented as a horror so totalizing that the gendered dimensions have been obscured. She notes that women's responsibilities for child rearing and caregiving make them especially susceptible to certain forms of harm that are inflicted on others *and* experienced as profound damage to oneself. As she argues, "Key to understanding the experience of women in the [Jewish] ghettos and camps is to see maternity infected by atrocity, where the established conventions of motherhood are deliberately ravaged and assaulted."[8] When survival may be predicated upon horrible moral dilemmas: What to do when mothers with young children were hurried to the gas chambers? Which child to save? How to swallow the grief of separation? How to live with choiceless choices? Understanding the gendered contours of caregiving is crucial to developing a vocabulary of violation that captures the continuity and magnification of each harmful act rather than seeing these as discrete wounds to body and soul.

The phrase "maternity infected by atrocity" is haunting. What of maternity conceived in rape and gestated in the toxic environment of war? There seems to be scant space for women to express the deep ambivalence that may accompany such pregnancies and the babies those violent acts may produce. In *Caring for Justice*, Robin West argues that more effort has been invested in the deployment of law as an instrument of redress than with a more fundamental set of questions: What does harm entail and how should we know it and recognize its manifestations? I recall when Ana Jara was installed as Peru's Minister for Women's Development on December 20, 2011. Shortly after her appointment, amid debates about legalizing abortion, she stated that raped women not only learn to live with their experiences but that the "super natural bond" between mother and child erases the violence by which the child was conceived. Welcome to the realm of magical thinking?

I imagine many women are ambivalent about pregnancy and mothering, even under the best of circumstances; and yet pathologizing maternal ambivalence is a leitmotif in parenting guides, public culture, and even in some of the literature on children born of wartime rape.[9] As Barbara Almond has written, maternal ambivalence is "that mixture of loving and hating feelings that all mothers experience toward their children, and the anxiety, shame, and guilt that the negative feelings engender in them."[10] Although these mixed emotions may in fact be common, many women are made to feel that those emotions are a personal failing rather than a more generalizable experience. Indeed, the late psychoanalyst Rozsika Parker argued that mothers have extremely limited room for the expression and working through of "inevitable maternal ambivalence" on both cultural and societal levels as well as internally due to the idealization of mothers in the symbolic register. She emphasized that becoming a mother inevitably entails dissonance and tension between the lived subjective experiences of mothering and the normative ideals of motherhood.[11] Recall the Colombian mothers who spoke about their children born of wartime rape: abort the baby, birth the baby, raise the child or put it up for adoption, love that child or hate it—"no importa lo que pase, todo el mundo echa la culpa a la madre" (no matter what, everyone blames the mother). The oppressive weight of hegemonic maternal scripts that place the burden to love on survivors of forced pregnancy and maternity should be considered as a potential form of gendered harm.

A leader in the field of gender and reparations is Ruth Rubio-Marín, whose work has focused on how to harness the transformative potential of reparations to destabilize gender hierarchies.[12] In part she advocates moving from a rights-based to a harms-based approach when designing reparations programs. As she argues, due to the gender bias of many rights systems, reparations (when conceived as redress for the violations of such rights) are likely to reproduce gender biases.[13] In contrast, focusing on "harms" can capture the wider range of consequences women disproportionately bear:

> Indeed, the need to identify who, beyond the right holder, has been individually or collectively affected by the violation and deserves redress allows movement beyond the rights paradigm in one concrete way that may be fundamental to women, namely by bringing to the fore the

interrelatedness of the harms and the ways in which the diffuse nature of harms affects women specifically. For instance, although, strictly speaking, there is no human right not to be widowed, the harm done to women whose husbands are executed or disappeared can nevertheless find adequate recognition through this harms-based notion of victim.[14]

Focusing on harms requires listening to women and to how they describe their experiences of sexual violence, forced pregnancy, maternity, mothering, mountains, water, and the long way around: in sum, listening to how women speak about fast and slow forms of violence that have placed them at the saturation point of interconnected and amplified insults and injuries.

FINAL REFLECTIONS

I began this book thinking about the legacies of war and a conundrum. The Women, Peace and Security Agenda has placed conflict-related sexual violence front and center on the international agenda; obscured is one potential consequence of sexual violence: children. With the aim of contributing to research on children born of wartime rape and sexual exploitation, I advocated moving beyond stigma to explanatory pluralism. It is clear from the literature and my own research that the logics of acceptance and rejection of the children and their mothers are granular and dynamic: they eschew any single story. I opted to explore entanglements that operate across multiple environments. Among those entanglements are names that locate these children within familial and communal histories of war, survival, brutality, and betrayal. The names are one component of the stories and silences that characterize postwar social landscapes. The social landscape at play here is peopled by, well, people . . . and many more living beings.

Troubled by the tendency to place the heavy lifting of reproductive labor on the shoulders of women, I next considered the multiple environments in which conception, pregnancy, and childbirth unfold, environments that may lie far beyond the control of any one woman, of any one person. From toxic chemicals to land mines, from rivers tinged with blood to angry mountains, the goal was to capture the multiple environments and actors that play a role in "distributed reproduction"—environments and actors that may in turn suffer various forms of reproductive violence.

An openness to the world and its capacity to "get under our skin" allowed me to draw connections between Indigenous epistemologies, situated biologies, and the burgeoning field of epigenetics. I questioned what is involved in "discovering" that our bodies bear life's signature upon them—or "discovering" that we share this world with more-than-human kin. The trope of discovery follows a particular history of modernity, settler colonialism, and capitalism: it is erected on the erasure of Indigenous and Native American peoples, their ways of life, and their theories about the world and the place of human beings in it. If there is to be a way forward on this planet, it will require moving beyond human exceptionalism and its devastating consequences.

Colombia's transitional justice process offers some movement in that direction. By recognizing the environment, "nature," as a victim of the armed conflict, Colombia opens up the possibility of a politics of accountability and coexistence that is not grounded in an anthropocentric rights framework. This framework can contribute to a new vocabulary of violation and of redress, a vocabulary that will also contribute to a gendered theory of harm. Entanglements and connectivity underscore that harms are not autonomous events separated by time and place; rather, there are saturation points that will occur along the fault lines of any given society. As Alaimo insists, exposure "is terribly uneven, across such simultaneously social and material categories as class, race, and the disparities between the global north and the global south."[1]

* * *

Let me return to *Fragmentos* and to another woman who spoke that afternoon. Maricela is a survivor-activist and a vocal advocate. She asked the audience to consider the myriad women in Colombia who live with *other* legacies of conflict-related sexual violence—incontinence, chronic sexually transmitted diseases, depression, post-traumatic stress syndrome—as well as those who were rendered sterile from the assault, the abortion, or the subsequent lack of medical attention. Those women may have no living children. Maricela considers herself fortunate to have a daughter, the product of her second rape and a witness to her third assault by paramilitaries. Her daughter and husband witnessed the gang rape; she told her masked assailants they could do "that to her," *provided they not so much as touch her daughter.* I can still hear the pride in her voice when recalling how she had protected her daughter. These are tales of tragedy, to be sure—tales of women who may enter old age with no adult children to care for them. That remains a primary "social security net" in many parts of the world. And yet these are also womanly narratives of heroism, endurance, outrage, struggle, and, at times, love.

It is time for collaborative research with these women, the fathers, and, when possible, their children. I suspect these children number in the hundreds of thousands, and we still know far too little about their lives and life chances. I have laid out some of the questions, offered with the conviction that combining ethnography, the environmental humanities, and epigenetics can lead to productive conversations. Perhaps these conversations can contribute to more hopeful legacies amid the long reach of war.

INTRODUCTION

1   Salcedo, November 7, 2019.
2   To read the full interview, see Rinaldi, "Peace Monument."
3   Unless otherwise noted, all translations are my own.
4   See Carpenter, *Born of War*.
5   Carpenter, *Born of War*, 4.
6   See Lock, "Comprehending the Body"; Clarkin, "Embodiment of War," 424.
7   See Crenshaw, *Demarginalizing the Intersection*; Crenshaw, "Mapping the Margins."
8   Adichie, "Danger of a Single Story."

CHAPTER ONE: BEYOND STIGMA

1   Preventing Sexual Violence in Conflict Initiative (PSVI), *Principles for Global Action: Preventing and Addressing Stigma Associated with Conflict-Related Sexual Violence*, https://assets.publishing.service.gov.uk/government/uploads/system/uploads /attachment_data/file/645636/PSVI_Principles_for_Global_Action.pdf.
2   See Hacking, "Looping Effects."
3   Theidon, "Hidden in Plain Sight," 194.
4   See Wood, "Variation in Sexual Violence during War," among others.
5   See Wood, "Variation in Sexual Violence during War."
6   See Mazurana, "Role of Spirituality."
7   This section draws upon my 2015 article "Hidden in Plain Sight."
8   See Theidon, *Entre prójimos*; Theidon, *Intimate Enemies*.
9   See Wood, "Variation in Sexual Violence during War," for a discussion of repertoires of violence.
10 For further discussion of children born of wartime rape in Peru, see Theidon, "Death of the Secret."
11 Das, *Life and Words*, 54.
12 Olivera Simic, personal communication, September 16, 2017.

13 Author's fieldwork, Colombia. The last two examples are quoted in Gómez Pava, "Daughters of the Sun."

14 Powell, "War Babies."

15 I thank Victoria Sanford for this information.

16 Smith, "Rape Victims' Babies."

17 Weitsman, "Politics of Identity."

18 Nowrojee, *Shattered Lives*, 39; Weitsman, "Politics of Identity," 577; Wax, "Rwandans Are Struggling."

19 Apio, "Uganda's Forgotten Children," 101.

20 McKelvey, *Dust of Life*; personal communication, University of Oregon, May 9, 2013.

21 Van Ee and Kleber, "Child in the Shadowlands," 643.

22 Vom Bruck and Bodenhorn, *Anthropology of Names*, 3.

23 I am influenced here by Stacy Alaimo and Donna Haraway, both of whom advocate that we turn our attention to entanglement and transcorporeality to move beyond human exceptionalism.

24 The Peruvian Truth and Reconciliation Commission (PTRC) determined that in certain times and places, the use of sexual violence by the armed forces was systematic (*Informe Final*, vol. 6). Peru's transitional justice project began in 2001 when the interim government of Valentín Paniagua established a Truth and Reconciliation Commission to investigate two decades of internal armed conflict (1980–2000) between guerrilla groups, the *rondas campesinas* (armed peasant patrols), and the Peruvian armed forces. The PTRC's mandate called for clarifying the processes, facts, and responsibilities of the violence and human rights violations during the internal armed conflict. When the PTRC concluded its two-year investigation in August 2003, it produced nine volumes consisting of eight thousand pages, based on almost seventeen thousand testimonies, fourteen public hearings, and hundreds of archives from not only the Peruvian government but also the US State Department. The PTRC estimated that approximately 69,280 people had been killed or disappeared, making it one of the country's most deadly conflicts. In the section of the *Informe Final* addressing the issue of accountability, the commissioners state that Sendero Luminoso (Shining Path) was responsible for 54 percent of the deaths and disappearances reported to the PTRC, and the armed forces were responsible for 37 percent. The PTRC confirmed that the casualties of the political violence were distributed by class and ethnicity, reporting that 75 percent of the dead and disappeared spoke a native language other than Spanish, and three out of every four people killed lived in a rural region and were farmers, poor, and illiterate. National indifference, especially among the powerful elite residing in urban centers, was greatly blamed for permitting this ethnic massacre. The literature is vast, but for more on gender, women's testimony, and the PTRC, see Bueno-Hansen, *Feminist and Human Rights Struggles*; Boesten, *Sexual Violence*; Henríquez Ayín, *Cuestiones de género*; and Theidon, *Intimate Enemies*. For more on the rise of Sendero Luminoso and the armed peasant patrols, see Gorriti, *Sendero*; and Degregori et al., *Las rondas campesinas*. For a historical perspective on

Ayacucho, where Sendero Luminoso began, see Heilman *Before the Shining Path*; and La Serna, *Corner of the Living.*

25 I cannot ascertain how widespread this practice was, and I only heard about this *after* the PTRC concluded its work. The communal authorities with whom my colleagues Edith Del Pino and Juan Yupanqui and I spoke indicated they had never told "this truth" during the Commission's work for fear they would be accused of a crime.

26 Taussig, *Defacement*, 2.

27 Apio, "Uganda's Forgotten Children," 101.

28 Apio, "Uganda's Forgotten Children," 101, emphasis added.

29 See Theidon, "Disarming the Subject"; Theidon, *Intimate Enemies*, 2012.

30 See Ní Aoláin, "Sex-Based Violence."

31 Baaz and Stern, *Sexual Violence as a Weapon of War?*

32 James Scott, *Seeing Like a State*, 71.

33 I refer here, of course, to Erving Goffman's work on stigma. He uses the term *moral career* to discuss the learning experience involved in managing a spoiled identity and the ongoing adjustments this experience places upon the self. Goffman, *Stigma*, 32–41.

34 "The idea that there is a 'proper' name (in the sense of being correct as well as being one's own) imbues the act of naming and the name itself with considerable moral force that reflects back on the name-giver as much as it influences the personhood of the name-receiver." Vom Bruck and Bodenhorn, *Anthropology of Names*, 11.

35 For a rich ethnographic analysis of Quechua speakers' encounters with personnel in the health post and the discriminatory treatment they experience, see Huayhua, "¿Runama Kani Icha Alquchu?" As Huayhua insightfully argues, however, these encounters are complicated negotiations in which both what it left unsaid or conveyed via body language speaks volumes about the ways in which subalterns attempt to manage the repressive apparatus of the state to their own ends—obviously on unequal terrain.

36 Macher, "Una práctica sistemática," 562.

37 Wiesse, "Manta de silencio," 61.

38 I have been asked who insisted on the names, the Civil Registrar or the women. Given that two last names must appear on the birth certificate, women may have been obligated to provide paternal last names that they had no way of knowing. Many soldiers adopted nicknames during their military service, such that the only "formal" name the women could provide to the Registrar was the rapist's military rank. I do, however, interpret these names within the framework of other women who told my colleagues and me that they considered these babies to be "children of the state," following a pattern of attempting to establish paternal responsibility.

39 Wiesse, "Manta de silencio," 58.

40 Wiesse, "Manta de silencio," 59.

41 Wiesse, "Manta de silencio," 60.

42 Chinese health official, quoted in Wee, "China Wants to Boost Births."

43 Grieg, *War Children*; Mochmann, "Children Born of War"; Seto, *No Place for a War Baby*; Lee and Bartels, "They Put a Few Coins."

44 Weitsman, "Politics of Identity," 566.

45 I met Samuel Munderere at a workshop on children born of wartime sexual violence that my colleague Dyan Mazurana and I convened at the Fletcher School in May 2018.

46 Nowrojee, *Shattered Lives*, 4.

47 See Anumol and Munderere, "Moving beyond Rwanda."

48 Anumol and Munderere, "Moving beyond Rwanda."

49 Anumol and Munderere, "Moving beyond Rwanda."

50 Denov et al., "Intergenerational Legacy," 10.

51 DeLaet, "Theorizing Justice for Children."

52 Denov, "Children Born of Wartime Rape."

53 See Tate, *Counting the Dead*, for a discussion of the United States' relationship with Colombian paramilitaries.

54 For more on the history of the paramilitaries, see Tate, *Drugs, Thugs, and Diplomats;* Romero Vidal, *Paramilitares y autodefensas;* García-Peña Jaramillo, "La relación del Estado colombiano"; and Cubides, "El poder paramilitar."

55 See Redacción Política, "¿Campaña de Uribe contra Gina Parody?"

56 Copy on file with author.

57 See Martínez Cortés, "Victims and Land Restitution."

58 Internal Displacement Monitoring Centre, "Colombia," accessed December 24, 2020, https://www.internal-displacement.org/countries/colombia.

59 See Cubides, "El poder paramilitar." For a discussion of internal forced displacement, see Molano, *Desterrados*.

60 Interviews, Red de Mujeres Profesionales y Víctimas.

61 I think here of Ní Aoláin's work on women during the Holocaust and the painful moral dilemmas of mothering during genocide. See Ní Aoláin, "Sex-Based Violence."

62 See Theidon, "Reconstructing Masculinities.".

63 United Nations, *Second Generation Disarmament*, 27–28.

64 LaPlante and Theidon, "Truth with Consequences"; de Greiff, *Handbook of Reparations*; Rubio-Marín, *What Happened*.

CHAPTER TWO: SITUATED BIOLOGIES

1 Evans-Campbell, "Historical Trauma," 317.

2 Brave Heart, "Wakiksuyapi," 247.

3 Evans-Campbell, "Historical Trauma," 326.

4 Kim TallBear (@KimTallBear), "The Atlantic with another #Settler Epiphany," Twitter, November 19, 2019, 9:45 a.m., https://twitter.com/KimTallBear/status /1196801697881837574.

5 Alaimo, *Exposed*, 155.

6 Niewöhner and Lock, "Situating Local Biologies"; Krieger, "Embodiment"; Lock, "Comprehending the Body." I do not want to homogenize Indigenous epistemolo-

gies, yet I do feel that across many contexts there is a shared element of human and more-than-human relatedness. As Maneesha Deckha argues, "Though mindful of the diversity reflected within and across Indigenous communities, it is still possible to comment on the multiple examples in Canada and throughout the globe of human Indigenous subjectivities being inseparable from non-human ones" ("Unsettling Anthropocentric Legal Systems," 84).

7   See Jennifer Scott at al., "Qualitative Analysis," 8.
8   See Engle, "Feminism and Its (Dis)Contents," 779.
9   Engle, "Feminism and Its (Dis)Contents," 784.
10 Weitsman, "Politics of Identity," 563.
11 Weitsman, "Politics of Identity," 565.
12 Weitsman, "Politics of Identity," 566.
13 Carpenter, "Surfacing Children."
14 Carpenter, "Surfacing Children," 447n106.
15 Carpenter, "Surfacing Children," 458n155, emphasis added.
16 Ross, *Understanding Reproductive Justice*.
17 Ross, *Understanding Reproductive Justice*, 2.
18 See Richards, *Fighting for the Rain Forest*, 8.
19 Zraly, Rubin, and Mukamana, "Motherhood and Resilience," 429.
20 Zraly, Rubin, and Mukamana, "Motherhood and Resilience," 428.
21 Jennifer Scott et al., "Qualitative Analysis," 7.
22 In her meta-analysis of rape across ninety-one major civil wars that occurred between 1980 and 2012, Dara Kay Cohen found great variation in the use, or not, of sexual violence; significantly, gang rape was more likely during armed conflict than during peacetime and more closely associated with armed state actors. This would also indicate forms of violence particular to armed conflict. Cohen, *Rape during Civil War*.
23 Wood, "Variation in Sexual Violence during War," 124–37.
24 Urban Walker, "Gender and Violence in Focus," 23.
25 Carpenter, *Forgetting Children Born*, 24.
26 Van Ee and Kleber, "Growing Up under a Shadow," 389
27 Jennifer Scott et al., "Qualitative Analysis," 3.
28 Jennifer Scott et al., "Qualitative Analysis," 3.
29 For a succinct assessment of the harmful effects of the Helms Amendment, see Barot, "Abortion Restrictions in U.S. Foreign Aid."
30 For a fascinating analysis of this public hearing and redemption via motherhood, see Bueno-Hansen, *Feminist and Human Rights Struggles*.
31 PTRC, *Informe Final*, 6:372, translation mine.
32 PTRC, *Informe Final*, 6:310. The pain of separation itself warrants further reflection; see "Sex-Based Violence," Ní Aoláin's analysis of gender-based violence during the Holocaust.
33 The classic ethnographic text challenging the maternal bonding literature is Scheper-Hughes, *Death without Weeping*.
34 Weitsman, "Politics of Identity," 577.

35 Jacqueline Murakatete, quoted in Theidon, "Death of the Secret."

36 Haraway, *Staying with the Trouble*, 30.

37 Alaimo has written extensively about exposure, by which she means an openness to the material world in which we are immersed. This term and her concept of "trans-corporeality" resonate with many Indigenous theories of being. See Alaimo, *Exposed*.

38 See Cielmecka and Asberg, "Toxic Embodiment," 101.

39 Women's Earth Alliance and Native Youth Sexual Health Network, "Violence on the Land," 2.

40 Women's Earth Alliance and Native Youth Sexual Health Network, "Violence on the Land," 50.

41 National Human Genome Research Institute, "The Human Genome Project," accessed May 27, 2021, https://www.genome.gov/human-genome-project.

42 See Karow, "Reading the Book of Life."

43 See Lock, "Lure of the Epigenome."

44 See Lock for "situated biologies," Niewohner for "embedded bodies," and Krieger for "embodiment," the last emphasizing how racism impacts bodies in lasting and harmful ways.

45 Niewöhner and Lock, "Situating Local Biologies," 688.

46 Clarkin, "Embodiment of War," 428–31.

47 Clarkin, "Embodiment of War," 423.

48 Richardson, "Maternal Bodies."

49 As Lynn Morgan and Elizabeth Roberts define it, "Reproductive governance refers to the mechanisms through which different historical configurations of actors—such as state, religious, and international financial institutions, NGOs, and social movements—use legislative controls, economic inducements, moral injunctions, direct coercion, and ethical incitements to produce, monitor, and control reproductive behaviours and population practices" ("Reproductive Governance," 243).

50 Hoke and McDade, "Biosocial Inheritance," 191.

51 Alaimo, *Exposed*, 185.

52 Murphy, "Distributed Reproduction."

CHAPTER THREE: ECOLOGIES AND AFTERMATHS

1 See H. Davis and Todd, "On the Importance of a Date, or Decolonizing the Anthropocene," 764.

2 See Haraway, *Staying with the Trouble*, for a sustained discussion of critters.

3 See TallBear, "Failed Settler Kinship, Truth and Reconciliation, and Science."

4 H. Davis and Todd, "On the Importance of a Date," 770.

5 See Nixon, *Slow Violence*.

6 For more on the history of the region, see Roldán, *Blood and Fire*; Uribe, *Urabá*; and Ballve, *Frontier Effect*, an insightful recent book that explores how the discourse of state absence and lawlessness produces a permanent "frontier effect."

7   See Judgement T-622/16, 2016.

8   María Cristina is a pseudonym. For a recent ethnography of the Peace Community San José de Apartadó, see Burnyeat, *Chocolate, Politics and Peace-Building*. I focus here on the Peace Communities, one of numerous local efforts to return and rebuild communities. Other efforts, beginning in 2003, include the "humanitarian zones" of Pueblo Nuevo (ninety families), Nueva Esperanza (forty-seven families), and Bella Flor (thirty families), which were created in Jiguamiandó. Three other zones, including El Tesoro and Las Camelias, were created in Curvaradó in 2006. As with the Peace Communities, the humanitarian zones are clearly demarcated areas inhabited by the civilian population where armed forces of any kind are not supposed to enter. In the zones, groups of families help each other to protect themselves against militarization while at the same time defending their rights. Since March 2005, these zones have the backing of the Inter-American Commission on Human Rights (IACHR), which has required the Colombian government to grant them special protection. As with many other state security efforts, this one has been poorly enforced.

9   I have referred to Father Leonides by his real name because he is a well-known public figure.

10 Bocarejo, "Ordinary Peace."

11 I have given my two colleagues pseudonyms to respect their privacy. Additionally, the analysis I present here is my own, based on extensive field notes and interviews.

12 The AUC was a coalition of paramilitary blocks.

13 Clarkin, "Embodiment of War," 423.

14 See Lock, "Lure of the Epigenome," on somatic determinism.

15 I think here of Elizabeth Roberts's innovative work in Mexico City. She is collaborating with a team of researchers studying the effects of chemical exposures, especially lead, on fetal and childhood growth and neurological development. She insists on the need to bring together biological and ethnographic data to produce more complex accounts of the links between ill-health and life circumstances. See Roberts, "Bio-ethnography."

16 Centro de Estudios para la Justicia Social Tierra Digna, *Risas, sueños y lamentos del río*, 13.

17 Centro de Estudios para la Justicia Social Tierra Digna, *Risas, sueños y lamentos del río.*

18 See Puig de la Bellacasa, *Matters of Care*, for a rich discussion of ethics in a posthumanist world.

19 Cunsolo and Ellis, "Ecological Grief," 275.

20 For a powerful visual essay on the land mines, see Nieves, "Legacy of Land Mines."

21 See Lyons, *Vital Decomposition*.

22 I borrow the term "warscape" from Nordstrom, *Different Kind*.

23 See Krystalli, "Narrating Victimhood."

24 Alcaldía Mayor de Bogotá D.C., "Decreto 4633 de 2011 Nivel Nacional," December 9, 2011, https://www.alcaldiabogota.gov.co/sisjur/normas/Norma1.jsp?i=44966.

25 Decree 4633, Article 3: "Para los pueblos indígenas el territorio es víctima, teniendo en cuenta su cosmovisión y el vínculo especial y colectivo que los une con la madre tierra."

26 Decree 4633, Article 45: "*Daño al territorio.* El territorio, comprendido como integridad viviente y sustento de la identidad y armonía, de acuerdo con la cosmovisión propia de los pueblos indígenas y en virtud del lazo especial y colectivo que sostienen con el mismo, sufre un daño cuando es violado o profanado por el conflicto armado interno y sus factores vinculados y subyacentes y vinculados."

27 Decree 4635, Article 40: "*Derecho fundamental al territorio.* La pervivencia de las comunidades entraña el ejercicio efectivo del derecho colectivo sobre sus territorios, en virtud de la estrecha relación cultural que mantienen con los mismos. El territorio es reconocido y comprendido como la base fundamental de sus culturas, su vida espiritual, su integridad y su desarrollo autónomo."

28 See Emblin, "Colombian Court Grants."

29 Emblin, "Colombian Court Grants."

30 Ximena González is a lawyer for Tierra Digna. See "We Are All Atrato River Guardians," n.d., https://www.tierradigna.org/pdfs/SomosGuardianesDelAtrato.pdf.

31 For further details, see JEP, "Comprehensive System of Truth, Justice Reparation and Non-repetition," 2019, https://www.jep.gov.co/Infografas/SIVJRNR_EN.pdf.

32 JEP, "Acuerdo no. 001 de 2018," March 9, 2018, https://www.jep.gov.co/salaplenajep/Acuerdo%20ASP%2001%20de%202018.pdf.

33 See Viaene, "Life Is Priceless," for a rich analysis of Mayan Q'echi theories of social healing.

34 For a discussion of counteragrarian reform, see Cubides, "El poder paramilitar."

35 Nixon, *Slow Violence*, 17.

36 See JEP, "Sala de reconocimiento de verdad, de responsabilidad y de determinación de los hechos y conductas Jurisdicción Especial para la Paz," May 24, 2018, https://www.jep.gov.co/Sala-de-Prensa/Documents/25.05.18%208pm%20SRVR%20GUIA%20para%20la%20elaboracion%20y%20presentacion%20de%20informes%20.pdf.

37 JEP, November 12, 2019, Decision 079, at 81.

38 See Nixon, *Slow Violence*, 40. Nixon draws upon Frantz Fanon's concepts of an army of cultural bewilderers and the important role they play under capitalism.

39 See Law 1448, Article 13. See also "Palabras de Monserrat Solano-Carboni, Representante Adjunta de la Oficina en Colombia del Alto Comisionado de las Naciones Unidas para los Derechos Humanos, en el evento Resolución 1325 en los conflictos emergentes," July 30, 2021, https://www.hchr.org.co/index.php/76-boletin/recursos/2470-ique-es-el-enfoque-diferencial; "¿Qué es enfoque diferencial?," YouTube, December 12, 2013, https://www.youtube.com/watch?v=WmoMp3Up35E 2013, produced by the República de Colombia Ministerio de Trabajo.

40 See Boellstorff, "Queer Studies," for a discussion of the "logic of enumeration."

41 See Lappé, Hein, and Landecker, "Environmental Politics."

42 See Agard-Jones, "Bodies in the System," for more on bodies as small places where larger systems of power manifest.

43 On the importance of measuring racism as a pathogen in its own right, see D. Davis, *Reproductive Injustice*; Krieger, "Embodiment."

44 Richardson, "Maternal Bodies," 222.

45 There is scant research on the fathers of children born of wartime rape, but that will change due to the pioneering work shown in Denov and Cadieux Van Vliet, "Missing Fathers"; and Oliveira and Baines, "Children 'Born of War.'"

46 Lorenzo, "At Standing Rock."

47 In this section, I draw upon Theidon, *Intimate Enemies*.

48 Theidon, "Anthropology and Transitional Justice."

49 Haraway, "Anthropocene, Capitalocene," 161.

CHAPTER FOUR: THE LONG WAY AROUND

1 I lived in a highland village for two years; this photo is not the village itself, as I wish to respect privacy. The photo does, however, depict the layout of the community and its surrounding geography very well.

2 I borrow Ní Aoláin's wonderful term "vocabulary of violation" from "Sex-Based Violence," 49.

3 Hayner, *Unspeakable Truths*.

4 Dyan Mazurana, personal communication, April 15, 2020.

5 Ní Aoláin, "Exploring a Feminist Theory of Harm," 218.

6 Ní Aoláin, "Exploring a Feminist Theory of Harm," 220.

7 Neenan, "Closing the Protection Gap," 12.

8 Ní Aoláin, "Sex-Based Violence," 52.

9 For example, see Van Ee and Kleber, "Growing Up under a Shadow," and the suggestion that "in a gentle fashion, the mother needs to be held accountable for her [indifferent] behavior" (390). It would be interesting to survey the extant maternal and child interventions for children born of wartime rape to determine the degree to which they are geared toward encouraging the mother to love and bond with her baby/child.

10 Almond, *Monster Within*, 2.

11 Benn, "Deep Maternal Alienation."

12 See Rubio-Marín, *What Happened*; Rubio-Marín, *Gender of Reparations*.

13 Rubio-Marín, *What Happened*, 31.

14 Rubio-Marín, *What Happened*, 31.

FINAL REFLECTIONS

1 Alaimo, *Exposed*, 185.

Adichie, Chimamanda Ngozi. "The Danger of a Single Story." TEDGlobal, July 2009. https://www.ted.com/talks/chimamanda_ngozi_adichie_the_danger_of_a_single _story?language=en.

Agard-Jones, Vanessa. "Bodies in the System." *Small Axe: A Caribbean Journal of Criticism* 17, no. 3 (42) (2013): 182–92.

Alaimo, Stacy. "Afterword: Crossing Time, Space, and Species." *Environmental Humanities* 11, no. 1 (2019): 239–41.

Alaimo, Stacy. *Exposed: Environmental Politics and Pleasures in Posthuman Times.* Minneapolis: University of Minnesota Press, 2016.

Almond, Barbara. *The Monster Within: The Hidden Side of Motherhood.* Berkeley: University of California Press, 2010.

Anumol, Dipali, and Samual Munderere. "Moving beyond Rwanda's 'Children of Bad Memory': A Conversation on Working with Mothers and Children Born of Wartime Rape." In *Challenging Conceptions: Children Born of Wartime Rape and Sexual Exploitation,* edited by Kimberly Theidon and Dyan Mazurana. New York: Oxford University Press, forthcoming.

Apio, Eunice. "Uganda's Forgotten Children of War." In *Born of War: Protecting Children of Sexual Violence Survivors in Conflict Zones,* edited by R. Charli Carpenter, 94–108. Bloomfield, CT: Kumarian, 2007.

Baaz, Maria Eriksson, and Maria Stern. *Sexual Violence as a Weapon of War? Perceptions, Prescriptions, Problems in the Congo and Beyond.* London: Zed, 2013.

Ballve, Teo. *The Frontier Effect: State Formation and Violence in Colombia.* Ithaca, NY: Cornell University Press, 2020.

Barot, Sneha. "Abortion Restrictions in U.S. Foreign Aid: The History and Harms of the Helms Amendment." *Guttmacher Policy Review* 16, no. 3 (2013). https://www .guttmacher.org/gpr/2013/09/abortion-restrictions-us-foreign-aid-history-and-harms -helms-amendment.

Benn, Melissa. "Deep Maternal Alienation." *Guardian,* October 27, 2006.

Bocarejo, Diana. "An Ordinary Peace in a Disparate Landscape of Longings." Hot Spots, *Fieldsights*, April 30, 2015. https://culanth.org/fieldsights/an-ordinary-peace-in -a-disparate-landscape-of-longings.

Boellstorff, Tom. "Queer Studies in the House of Anthropology." *Annual Review of Anthropology* 36 (2007): 17–35.

Boesten, Jelke. *Sexual Violence during War and Peace: Gender, Power, and Post-conflict Justice in Peru*. London: Palgrave Macmillan, 2014.

Brave Heart, Maria Yellow Horse. "Wakiksuyapi: Carrying the Historical Trauma of the Lakota." *Tulane Studies in Social Welfare* 21, no. 22 (2000): 245–66.

Bueno-Hansen, Pascha. *Feminist and Human Rights Struggles in Peru: Decolonizing Transitional Justice*. Urbana: University of Illinois Press, 2015.

Burnyeat, Gwen. *Chocolate, Politics and Peace-Building: An Ethnography of the Peace Community of San José de Apartadó*. London: Palgrave Macmillan, 2018.

Calle, Helena. "La JEP reconoce que la naturaleza es víctima del conflict." *El Spectador*, February 5, 2020. https://www.elespectador.com/noticias/medio-ambiente/la-jep -reconoce-que-la-naturaleza-es-victima-del-conflicto-articulo-903153.

Carpenter, Charli R. *Born of War: Protecting Children of Sexual Violence Survivors in Conflict Zones*. Bloomfield, CT: Kumarian, 2007.

Carpenter, Charli R. *Forgetting Children Born of War: Setting the Human Rights Agenda in Bosnia and Beyond*. New York: Columbia University Press, 2010.

Carpenter, Charli R. "Surfacing Children: Limitations of Genocidal Rape Discourse." *Human Rights Quarterly* 22, no. 2 (2000): 428–77.

Centro de Estudios para la Justicia Social Tierra Digna. *Risas, sueños y lamentos del río: Vivencias de los ríos Atrato y Baudó desde la mirada de sus guardianas*. Bogotá: Tierra Digna, 2019.

Cielmecka, Olga, and Cecilia Asberg. "Toxic Embodiment and Feminist Environmental Humanities." *Environmental Humanities* 11, no. 1 (2019): 101–7.

Clarkin, Patrick F. "The Embodiment of War: Growth, Development, and Armed Conflict." *Annual Review of Anthropology* 48 (2019): 423–42.

Cohen, Dara Kay. *Rape during Civil War*. Ithaca, NY: Cornell University Press, 2016.

Crenshaw, Kimberlé. *Demarginalizing the Intersection of Race and Sex: A Black Feminist Critique of Antidiscrimination Doctrine, Feminist Theory and Antiracist Politics*. Chicago: University of Chicago Legal Forum, 1989.

Crenshaw, Kimberlé. "Mapping the Margins: Intersectionality, Identity Politics, and Violence against Women of Color." *Stanford Law Review* 43 (1993): 1241–99.

Cubides, Fernando. "Narcotráfico y paramilitarismo: Una matrimonia indisolble." In *El poder paramilitar*, edited by Alfredo Rangel, 205–69. Bogotá: Planeta Colombia, 2005.

Cunsolo, Ashlee, and Neville R. Ellis. "Ecological Grief as a Mental Health Response to Climate Change–Related Loss." *Nature Climate Change* 8 (2018): 275–81.

Das, Veena. *Life and Words: Violence and the Descent into the Ordinary*. Berkeley: University of California Press, 2006.

Davis, Dána-Ain. *Reproductive Injustice: Racism, Pregnancy, and Premature Birth*. New York: New York University Press, 2019.

Davis, Heather, and Zoe Todd. "On the Importance of a Date, or Decolonizing the Anthropocene." *ACME: An International Journal for Critical Geographies* 16, no. 4 (2017): 761–80.

Deckha, Maneesha. "Unsettling Anthropocentric Legal Systems: Reconciliation, Indigenous Laws, and Animal Personhood." *Journal of Intercultural Studies* 41, no. 1 (2020): 77–97.

Degregori, Carlos Iván, ed. *Las rondas campesinas y la derrota de Sendero Luminoso*. Lima: Institute de Estudios Peruanos, 1996.

de Greiff, Pablo, ed. *The Handbook of Reparations*. Oxford: Oxford University Press, 2008.

DeLaet, Debra. "Theorizing Justice for Children Born of War." In *Born of War: Protecting Children of Sexual Violence Survivors in Conflict Zones*, edited by R. Charli Carpenter, 128–48. Bloomfield, CT: Kumarian, 2007.

Denov, Myriam. "Children Born of Wartime Rape: The Intergenerational Realities of Sexual Violence and Abuse." *Ethics, Medicine and Public Health* 1, no. 1 (2015): 61–68.

Denov, Myriam, and Anaïs Cadieux Van Vliet. "Missing Fathers: Children Born of Wartime Rape and Their Perspectives on Fathers and Fatherhood in Northern Uganda." In *Challenging Conceptions: Children Born of Wartime Rape and Sexual Exploitation*, edited by Kimberly Theidon and Dyan Mazurana. New York: Oxford University Press, forthcoming.

Denov, Myriam, Leah Woolner, Jules Pacifique Bahati, Paulin Nsuki, and Obed Shyaka. "The Intergenerational Legacy of Genocidal Rape: The Realities and Perspectives of Children Born of the Rwandan Genocide." *Journal of Interpersonal Violence*, May 15, 2017, 1–22.

Duggan, Colleen, Claudia Paz y Paz Bailey, and Julie Guillerot. "Reparations for Sexual and Reproductive Violence: Prospects for Achieving Gender Justice in Guatemala and Peru." *International Journal of Transitional Justice* 2, no. 2 (2008): 192–213.

Emblin, Richard. "A Colombian Court Grants the Altrato River Constitutional Rights." *City Paper*, June 8, 2017. http://thecitypaperbogota.com/news/a-colombian-court-gives-the-atrato-river-constitutional-rights/17311.

Engle, Karen. "Feminism and Its (Dis)Contents: Criminalizing Wartime Rape in Bosnia and Herzegovina." *American Journal of International Law* 99, no. 4 (2005): 778–816.

Evans-Campbell, Teresa. "Historical Trauma in American Indian/Native Alaska Communities: A Multilevel Framework for Exploring Impacts on Individuals, Families, and Communities." *Journal of Interpersonal Violence* 23, no. 3 (2008): 316–38.

García-Peña Jaramillo, Daniel. "La relación del Estado colombiano con el fenómeno paramilitary: por el esclarecimiento histórico." *Análisis Político*, no. 53, (2005): 58–76.

Goffman, Erving. *Stigma: Notes on the Management of Spoiled Identity*. New York: Pelican Books, 1968.

Gómez Pava, Vilma Amparo. "The Daughters of the Sun in the Land of the Jaguars." Defense for Children International, Bogotá, Colombia, 2014.

Gorriti, Gustavo. *Sendero: Historia de la Guerra milenaria en el Perú*. Lima: Editorial Planeta Perí, 1990.

Grieg, Kai. *The War Children of the World*. Bergen, Norway: War and Children Identity Project, 2001.

Grimard, F., and S. Laszlo. "Long-Term Effects of Civil Conflict on Women's Health Outcomes in Peru." *World Development* 54 (February 2014): 139–55.

Hacking, I. "The Looping Effects of Human Kinds." In *Causal Cognition: A Multidisciplinary Debate: A Fyssen Foundation Symposium*, edited by D. Sperber, D. Premack, and A. J. Premack, 351–94. New York: Clarendon, 1995.

Haraway, Donna. "Anthropocene, Capitalocene, Plantationcene, Chthulucene: Making Kin." *Environmental Humanities* 6 (2015): 159–65.

Haraway, Donna. *Staying with the Trouble: Making Kin in the Chthulucene*. Durham, NC: Duke University Press, 2016.

Hayner, Priscilla. *Unspeakable Truths: Transitional Justice and the Challenge of Truth Commissions*. 2nd ed. London: Routledge, 2010.

Heilman, Jaymie. *Before the Shining Path: Politics in Rural Ayacucho, 1895–1980*. Palo Alto, CA: Stanford University Press, 2010.

Henríquez Ayín, Narda. *Cuestiones de género y poder en el conflicto armado en el Perú*. Lima, Peru: CONCYTEC, 2006.

Hoke, Morgan K., and Thomas McDade. "Biosocial Inheritance: A Framework for the Study of the Intergenerational Transmission of Health Disparities." *Annals of Anthropological Practice* 38, no. 2 (2014): 187–213.

Huayhua, Margarita. "¿Runama Kani Icha Alquchu? Everyday Discrimination in the Southern Andes." PhD diss., University of Michigan, 2010.

Karow, Julie. "Reading the Book of Life." *Scientific American*, February 12, 2001. https://www.scientificamerican.com/article/reading-the-book-of-life/.

Krieger, Nancy. "Embodiment: A Conceptual Glossary for Epidemiology." *Journal of Epidemiology and Community Health* 59 (2005): 350–55.

Krystalli, Roxani. "Narrating Victimhood: Dilemmas and (In)Dignities." *International Journal of Feminist Politics* 23, no. 1 (2021): 125–46.

LaPlante, Lisa, and Kimberly Theidon. "Truth with Consequences: The Politics of Reparations in Post–Truth Commission Peru." *Human Rights Quarterly* 29, no. 1 (2007): 228–50.

Lappé, Martine, Robbin Jeffries Hein, and Hannah Landecker. "Environmental Politics of Reproduction." *Annual Review of Anthropology* 48 (October 2019): 133–50.

LaSerna, Miguel. *The Corner of the Living: Ayacucho on the Eve of the Shining Path Insurgency*. Chapel Hill: University of North Carolina Press, 2012.

Lathrop, Anthony. "Pregnancy Resulting from Rape." *JOGNN: Principles and Practice* 27, no. 1 (January 1, 1998): 25–31.

Lee, Sabine, and Susan Bartels. "'They Put a Few Coins in Your Hand to Drop a Baby in You': A Study of Peacekeeper-Fathered Children in Haiti." *International Peacekeeping* 27, no. 2 (2019): 177–209.

Lock, Margaret. "The Lure of the Epigenome." *Lancet* 381, no. 9881 (2013): 1896–97.

Lock, Margaret. "Comprehending the Body in the Era of the Epigenome." *Current Anthropology* 56, no. 2 (2015): 151–77.

Lorenzo, Rachel. "At Standing Rock, Environmental Justice Is Reproductive Justice." *Rewire*, September 20, 2016. https://rewire.news/article/2016/09/20/standing-rock-environmental-justice-reproductive-justice/.

Lyons, Kristina. *Vital Decomposition: Soil Practitioners and Life Politics*. Durham, NC: Duke University Press, 2020.

Macher, Sofía. "Una práctica sistemática y generalizada." *Ideele*, no. 169 (April 2005): 562–63.

Martínez Cortés, Paula. "The Victims and Land Restitution Law in Colombia in Context: An Analysis of the Contradictions between the Agrarian Model and Compensation for the Victims." Forschungs- und Dokumentationszentrum Chile-Lateinamerika (FDCL) and Transnational Institute (TNI), December 2013.

Mazurana, Dyan. "The Role of Spirituality and Ritual in the Acceptance of Children Born of Conflict-Related Sexual Violence." In *Challenging Conceptions: Children Born of Wartime Rape and Sexual Exploitation*, edited by Kimberly Theidon and Dyan Mazurana. New York: Oxford University Press, forthcoming.

McKelvey, Robert S. *The Dust of Life: America's Children Abandoned in Vietnam*. Seattle: University of Washington Press, 1999.

Mochmann, Ingvill C. "Children Born of War—A Decade of International and Inter-disciplinary Research." *Historical Social Research / Historische Sozialforschung* 42, no. 1 (159) (2017): 320–46.

Molano, Alfredo. *Desterrados: Crónicas del desarraigo*. Bogotá: Punta de Lectura, 2001.

Morgan, Lynn M., and Elizabeth F. S. Roberts. "Reproductive Governance in Latin America." *Anthropology and Medicine* 19, no. 2 (2012): 241–54.

Murphy, Michelle. "Distributed Reproduction, Chemical Violence, and Latency." *Scholar and Feminist Online* 11, no. 3 (2013).

Neenan, Joanne. "Closing the Protection Gap for Children Born of War: Addressing Stigmatisation and the Intergenerational Impact of Sexual Violence in Conflict." Centre for Women, Peace and Security, London School of Economics, 2017.

Ní Aoláin, Fionnuala. "Exploring a Feminist Theory of Harm in the Context of Conflicted and Post-conflict Societies." *Queen's Law Journal* 35 (2009): 219–44.

Ní Aoláin, Fionnuala. "Sex-Based Violence and the Holocaust—A Reevaluation of Harms and Rights in International Law." *Yale Journal of Law and Feminism* 12, no. 43 (2000): 42–84.

Nieves, Evelyn. "A Legacy of Land Mines in Colombia." *New York Times*, October 28, 2015.

Niewöhner, Jörg, and Margaret Lock. "Situating Local Biologies: Anthropological Perspectives on Environment/Human Entanglements." *BioSocieties* 13, no. 4 (2018): 681–97.

Nixon, Rob. *Slow Violence and the Environmentalism of the Poor*. Cambridge, MA: Harvard University Press, 2011.

Nordstrom, Carolyn. *A Different Kind of War Story*. Philadelphia: University of Pennsylvania Press, 1997.

Nowrojee, Binaifer. *Shattered Lives: Sexual Violence during the Rwandan Genocide and Its Aftermath*. New York: Human Rights Watch, 1996.

Oliveira, Camile, and Erin Baines. "Children 'Born of War': A Role for Fathers?" *International Affairs* 96, no. 2 (2020): 439–55.

Peruvian Truth and Reconciliation Commission (PTRC). *Informe Final*. Lima: Peruvian Truth and Reconciliation Commission, 2003.

Powell, Siam. "War Babies." *Weekend Australian*, March 10, 2001.

Puig de la Bellacasa, María. *Matters of Care: Speculative Ethics in More Than Human Worlds*. Minneapolis: University of Minnesota Press, 2017.

Redacción Política. "¿Campaña de Uribe contra Gina Parody?" *El Spectador*, August 8, 2016. https://www.elespectador.com/noticias/politica/campana-de-uribe-contra-gina-parody-articulo-647943/.

Richards, Paul. *Fighting for the Rain Forest: War, Youth and Resources in Sierra Leone*. New York: Oxford University Press, 1996.

Richardson, Sarah S. "Maternal Bodies in the Postgenomic Order: Gender and the Explanatory Landscape of Epigenetics." In *Postgenomics: Perspectives on Biology after the Genome*, edited by Sarah S. Richardson and Hallam Stevens, 210–31. Durham, NC: Duke University Press, 2015.

Rinaldi, Ray Mark. "A Peace Monument in Colombia Is Caught in a New Crossfire." *New York Times*, October 23, 2019.

Roberts, Elizabeth, F. S. "Bio-ethnography: A Collaborative, Methodological Experiment in Mexico City." *Somatosphere*, February 26, 2015. http://somatosphere.net/2015/bio-ethnography.html/.

Roldán, Mary. *Blood and Fire: La Violencia in Antioquia, Colombia*. Durham, NC: Duke University Press, 2002.

Romero Vidal, Mauricio. *Paramilitares y autodefensas: 1982–2003*. Bogotá: Editorial Planeta Colombiano, 2003.

Ross, Loretta J. *Understanding Reproductive Justice*. Atlanta: Sister Song Women of Color Reproductive Health Collective, 2006.

Rubio-Marín, Ruth, ed. *The Gender of Reparations: Unsettling Sexual Hierarchies while Redressing Human Rights Violations*. Cambridge: Cambridge University Press, 2009.

Rubio-Marín, Ruth, ed. *What Happened to the Women? Gender and Reparations for Human Rights Violations*. New York: Social Science Research Council, 2006.

Sanchez Parra, Tatiana. "The Hollow Shell: Children Born of War and the Realities of the Armed Conflict in Colombia." *International Journal of Transitional Justice* 12, no. 1 (2018): 45–63.

Sanchez Parra, Tatiana. "Searching for a Spectre: Victimhood and the Ghost of Children Born of War in Colombia." In *Challenging Conceptions: Children Born of Wartime Rape and Sexual Exploitation*, edited by Kimberly Theidon and Dyan Mazurana. New York: Oxford University Press, forthcoming.

Scheper-Hughes, Nancy. *Death without Weeping: The Violence of Everyday Life in Brazil*. Berkeley: University of California Press, 1995.

Scott, James. *Seeing Like a State: How Schemes to Improve the Human Condition Have Failed*. New Haven, CT: Yale University Press, 1998.

Scott, Jennifer, et al. "A Qualitative Analysis of Decision-Making among Women with Sexual Violence-Related Pregnancies in Conflict-Affected Eastern Democratic Republic of the Congo." *BMC Pregnancy and Childbirth* 18, no. 1 (2018): 1–9.

Seto, Donna. *No Place for a War Baby: The Global Politics of Children Born of Wartime Sexual Violence*. London: Routledge, 2013.

Silva Santisteban Manrique, Rocio. *El factor asco: Discursos autoritarios y basurización simbólica en el Perú contemporaneo*. Lima: Red de Ciencias Sociales / Instituto de Estudios Peruanos, 2009.

Smith, Helena. "Rape Victims' Babies Pay the Price of War." *Observer*, April 16, 2000.

TallBear, Kim. "Failed Settler Kinship, Truth and Reconciliation, and Science." Indigenous Science, Technology, and Society, 2016. https://indigenoussts.com/failed-settler-kinship-truth-and-reconciliation-and-science/.

Tate, Winifred. *Counting the Dead: The Culture and Politics of Human Rights Activism in Colombia*. Berkeley: University of California Press, 2007.

Tate, Winifred. *Drugs, Thugs, and Diplomats: U.S. Policymaking in Colombia*. Palo Alto, CA: Stanford University Press, 2015.

Taussig, Michael. *Defacement: Public Secrecy and the Labor of the Negative*. Stanford, CA: Stanford University Press, 1999.

Theidon, Kimberly. "Anthropology and Transitional Justice." In *International Encyclopedia of Anthropology*, edited by Hilary Callan. Malden, MA: Wiley-Blackwell, 2018.

Theidon, Kimberly. "The Death of the Secret: Public and Private in Anthropology." Wenner-Gren Symposium 149, March 14–20, Sintra, Portugal, 2014.

Theidon, Kimberly. "Disarming the Subject: Remembering War and Imagining Citizenship in Peru." *Cultural Critique*, no. 54 (2003): 67–87.

Theidon, Kimberly. *Entre prójimos: El conflicto armado interno y la política de la reconciliación en el Perú*. Lima: Instituto de Estudios Peruanos, 2004.

Theidon, Kimberly. "From Guns to God: Mobilizing Evangelical Christianity in Urabá, Colombia." In *Religious Responses to Violence: Human Rights in Latin America Past and Present*, edited by Alexander Wilde, 443–476. North Bend: University of Notre Dame, 2015.

Theidon, Kimberly. "Hidden in Plain Sight: Children Born of Wartime Sexual Violence." *Current Anthropology* 56, no. S12 (2015): 191–200.

Theidon, Kimberly. *Intimate Enemies: Violence and Reconciliation in Peru*. Philadelphia: University of Pennsylvania Press, 2013.

Theidon, Kimberly. "Reconstructing Masculinities: The Disarmament, Demobilization, and Reintegration of Former Combatants in Colombia." *Human Rights Quarterly* 31, no. 1 (2009): 1–34.

Thouin, Hugues, Lydie Le Forestier, Pascale Gautret, Daniel Hubé, Valérie Laperche, Sebastien Dupraz, and Fabienne Battaglia-Brunet. "Characterization and Mobility of Arsenic and Heavy Metals in Soils Polluted by the Destruction of Arsenic-Containing Shells from the Great War." *Science of the Total Environment* 550 (April 15, 2016): 658–69.

Tsing, Anna Lowenhaupt. *The Mushroom at the End of the World: On the Possibility of Life in Capitalist Ruins*. Princeton, NJ: Princeton University Press, 2015.

United Nations. *Second Generation Disarmament, Demobilization and Reintegration Practice and Peace Operations: A Contribution to the New Horizon Discussion on Challenges and Opportunities for UN Peacekeeping*. New York: United Nations, 2010.

Urban Walker, Margaret. "Gender and Violence in Focus: A Background for Gender Justice in Reparations." In *The Gender of Reparations: Unsettling Sexual Hierarchies while*

Redressing Human Rights Violations, edited by Ruth Rubio-Marín, 18–62. Cambridge: Cambridge University Press, 2009.

Uribe, María Teresa. *Urabá: ¿Región o territorio? Un análisis en el contexto de la política, las historia, y la etnicidad*. Medellín: INER-Corpourabá, 1992.

van Ee, Elisa, and Rolf J. Kleber. "Child in the Shadowlands." *Lancet* 380, no. 9842 (2012): 642–43.

van Ee, Elisa, and Rolf J. Kleber. "Growing Up under a Shadow: Key Issues in Research on and Treatment of Children Born of Rape." *Child Abuse Review* 22 (2013): 386–97.

Viaene, Lieselotte. "Life Is Priceless: Mayan Q'Eqchi' Voices on the Guatemalan National Reparations Program." *International Journal of Transitional Justice* 4, no. 1 (2010): 4–25.

Vom Bruck, Gabriele, and Barbara Bodenhorn, eds. *The Anthropology of Names and Naming*. New York: Cambridge University Press, 2006.

Wax, Emily. "Rwandans Are Struggling to Love Children of Hate." *Washington Post*, March 28, 2004.

Wee, Sui-Lee. "China Wants to Boost Births. But It's Wary of Losing Control." *New York Times*, May 12, 2021.

Weitsman, Patricia. "Children Born of War and the Politics of Identity." In *Born of War: Protecting Children of Sexual Violence Survivors in Conflict Zones*, edited by Charli Carpenter, 110–28. Bloomfield, CT: Kumarian, 2007.

Weitsman, Patricia. "The Politics of Identity and Sexual Violence: A Review of Bosnia and Rwanda." *Human Rights Quarterly* 30, no. 3 (2008): 561–78.

West, Robin. *Caring for Justice*. New York: New York University Press, 1999.

Wiesse, Patricia. "Manta de silencio." *Ideele*, no. 169 (April 2005): 59–61.

Wood, Elisabeth. "Variation in Sexual Violence during War." *Politics and Society* 34 no. 3 (2006): 307–42

Wood, Elisabeth. "Armed Groups and Sexual Violence: When Is Wartime Rape Rare?" *Politics and Society* 37, no. 1 (2009): 131–61.

Women's Earth Alliance and Native Youth Sexual Health Network. "Violence on the Land, Violence on Our Bodies: Building an Indigenous Response to Environmental Violence." Report and Toolkit, 2016. http://landbodydefense.org/uploads/files/VLVBReportToolkit2016.pdf.

Zraly, Maggie, Sarah E. Rubin, and Donatilla Mukamana. "Motherhood and Resilience among Rwandan Genocide-Rape Survivors." *Ethos* 41, no. 4 (2013): 411–39.

Engle, Karen, 42

entanglements, 13–19, 93–94; interspecies, 6–7, 15, 40, 53, 58, 74–75; naming practices and children born of sexual violence, 15–19, 93–94; Peru's environmental entanglements, 15–16; war and, 15

Entre prójimos (Theidon), 38–39

environments and legacies of armed conflicts, 6–7, 57–84, 94; Colombia's Atrato River declared victim of war, 7, 59, 76–77; Colombia's recognition of environmental impact of war, 7, 59, 75–82, 94; and "distributed reproduction," 55, 79, 81, 94; ecocide and genocide, 58; ecological grief, 74; environmental racism, 53; environmental reproductive justice, 81–84; Eurocentric concept of the Anthropocene, 58; exposure and epigenetics, 53–55, 73–74; interspecies entanglements (relations between human and more-than-human), 6–7, 15, 40, 53, 58, 74–75; maternal environments, 53–55, 73–74, 81–82; and "vernacular landscapes," 78; witchcraft and illnesses in Peru's highlands, 82–83. *See also* situated biologies

Eperara Siapiadaara people of Colombia, 79

epigenetics, 40, 53–55, 73–74; and environmental reproductive justice, 81; and ethnographic research, 73–74, 103n15; focusing on maternal bodies and environments, 53–55, 73–74; intergenerational research on impact of war stressors, 54, 73–74; and paternal transmission, 54–55, 81

ethnography of postconflict settings, feminist, 13–14, 46–48, 55, 73–74, 95; comparative research on injurious names in postconflict settings, 13–14; "continuum of violence" approach, 47–48; epigenetics and, 55, 73–74, 103n15; studying how women talk about sexual violence, 46–48

exposure: Alaimo on, 94, 102n37; maternal environments, war, and epigenetics, 53–55, 73–74; and ontological entanglement with the environment, 53; and paternal transmission and epigenetics, 81

extractive industries: and Colombia's oil resources, 60, 78; petrocapitalism, 58

feminist scholarship: challenge to "weapon of war" approach to rape, 19; critiques of law and liberalism that fail to capture experiences of women, 89; and environmental reproductive justice, 81–82; ethnography of postconflict settings, 13–14, 46–48, 55, 73–74, 95; gendered identities as social creations, 30; on genocide and rape, 42; and international agenda's attention to children born of wartime rape, 5

Fragmentos (Salcedo's art installation and "anti-monument" in Bogotá), 1–2, 94–95

Fuerzas Armadas Revolucionarias de Colombia (FARC, Revolutionary Armed Forces of Colombia): Atrato River blockades, 65, 67–68, 72; and Colombia's civil war, 26–27; origins and Marxist ideology, 26; and the 2016 Peace Accords, 1, 28–30, 77; and Urabá region Peace Communities, 66–69; Urabá region violence and struggles for control, 60–73

Gamboa García, Georgina, 50–51

gang rape and war, 101n22; Colombia, 95; Peru, 16, 21–22, 44; pregnancies resulting from, 21–22, 50–52; Rwanda, 47; women's shame, 47

gendered theory of harm, 85–92, 94; designing reparations programs from a harms-based approach, 91–92; forms of harm that are illegible in traditional international law, 89–90; and gender biases in reparations programs, 89, 91–92; and gendered contours of child rearing and caregiving, 90; gendered dimensions of mountains, drinking water, and steep paths (story of Ayacucho, Peru), 86–88; and legal procedures for redress that fail to ask questions about maternal ambivalence, 90–91; Ní Aoláin on the "problem of capture," 89; and other legacies of conflict-related sexual violence, 94–95; and ways other than sexual violence in which girls and women experience war, 89–90

Geneva Conventions, 4

global gag rule (Mexico City policy), 49–50

Goffman, Erving, 99n33

Hacking, Ian, 10

Haraway, Donna, 53, 84

harms-based approaches, 91–92. *See also* gendered theory of harm

Hayner, Priscilla, 88

Hein, Robin Jeffries, 81

Helms, Jesse, 50

Helms Amendment, 49–50

Herero genocide (early 1900s), 57

heroism, narratives of women's, 43–45, 95

"Hidden in Plain Sight" (Theidon), 10

Hoke, Morgan, 55

Holocaust, 54, 57, 90

Hualla, Peru, 43–44

Huanta, Peru, 39, 87, 88

Huayhua, Margarita, 99n35

Human Genome Project (HGP), 53–54

Human Rights Watch (HRW), 29

Indigenous peoples: and the Anthropocene, 58; and Colombia's JEP investigations of crimes against, 76–79; Colombia's Ley de Víctimas (Law 1448) and Decrees detailing rights of, 76, 104n25, 104n26, 104n27; concept of historical

Peruvian Truth and Reconciliation Commission (PTRC) (Comisión de la Verdad y Reconciliación del Perú, CVR), 17, 21–22, 50–52, 98n24; *casos judicializables* for further investigation, 21; *estudios en profundidad* (detailed case studies), 21; *Informe Final*, 51, 98n24; investigations of pregnancies resulting from wartime rape, 51–52; women's testimonies, 17, 20, 50–52
petrocapitalism, 58
Plan International, 24
poverty: Colombia's reparations program and disclosure dilemmas for poor women, 33; role of Colombia's war in production of, 72–73
Prime Minister's Special Representative on Preventing Sexual Violence in Conflict (UK), 9
Principles for Global Action (UK), 9–10
"problem of capture," 89
"psychosocial activities": and Colombian survivors of sexual violence, 33–35; former combatants in Colombia, 33–34, 35

Quechua-speaking communities in Peru: Ayacucho, 7, 16, 18, 37–39, 51–52, 86–88; *ayni* and *aynicha* (reciprocal labor exchanges) and sexual violence on military bases, 16; *chiki* (danger), 13; children's emotional education and "kuyachicuyta yachana" (learning how to make others love you), 52; encounters with government personnel, 99n35; environmental and social legacies of internal armed conflict, 37–39; *llakis*, 38, 49; *mal de rabia*, 38; *mancharisqa ñuñu* ("la teta asustada") and women's concerns about breast milk and transmission of suffering, 38–39; military bases, 16, 21–22, 43, 83, 86–88; rape victims' attempted abortions and infanticides, 48–49; *regla blanca*, 38; on *sasachakuy tiempo* (the difficult time/the war years), 15, 39; Umaru, 38; *waqcha* and children born of war, 7–8; women's bodies as sites of traumatic memories, 38–39; women's memory afflictions (toxic memories), 38–39, 49

Reagan, Ronald, 49
los regalos de los soldados (the soldiers' gifts), 13, 14, 20
reparations: Colombia's campesinos' demand for "moral reparation," 62–63; Colombia's land reparations, 76; Colombia's program for children born of sexual violence, 6, 30–35; Colombia's recognition of environmental legacies of war, 75–82, 94; gender biases and, 89, 91–92; harms-based approaches, 91–92; implementation and distribution challenges in Colombia, 31–34; issues of disclosure, 31–35; as staple of transitional justice processes, 88–89
"repertoires of violence," 10–11, 47

reproductive governance, 20, 55, 102n49
reproductive justice, 46, 81–84; abortion and, 5, 46, 49–50, 89–90; African American women and, 46; and "distributed reproduction," 55, 79, 81, 94; effects of global gag rule (Mexico City policy) and Helms Amendment, 49–50; environmental, 81–84; and reproductive governance, 55, 102n49
resilience, maternal, 47
Richards, Paul, 46
Richardson, Sarah, 54–55, 81
Rivera, Leonor, 46
Roberts, Elizabeth, 102n49, 103n15
Rome Statute of the International Criminal Court, 4
Rubin, Sarah, 47
Rubio-Marín, Ruth, 91–92
Rwanda, post-genocide, 3–4, 14, 23–26; assumptions that children born of rape are biologically associated with the enemy, 41; birth certificates and disclosure challenges for children born of rape, 23–26; International Criminal Tribunal, 3–4; research on relationships between mothers and children born of rape, 47, 52; work of Samuel Munderere and SURF with women survivors and children born of rape, 23–25

Salcedo, Doris, 1–2
Santa Fe de Ralito I agreement (2003), 28
Santos, Juan Manuel, 28–31, 76, 78
Scott, Jennifer, 41, 47, 49
Sendero Luminoso (Shining Path), 20, 41–42, 43, 51, 98n24
settler colonialism, 39–40, 57, 58, 80, 94
Shattered Lives (Nowrojee), 41
Sistema Integral de Verdad, Justicia, Reparación y No Repetición (SIVJRNR, Comprehensive System of Truth, Justice, Reparation and Non-repetition), 77
situated biologies, 6, 37–55; abortion and rape-related pregnancies, 2–3, 41, 45–46, 47, 48–50; children in utero when their mothers were raped, 51–52; and "continuum of violence" approach, 47–48; epigenetics, 40, 53–55, 73–74; intellectual disabilities and children of rape, 3, 37, 48–49, 52; mother's love and children born of rape, 11–12, 52–53, 91; patriarchal biologies and theories of transmission, 6, 11, 40–43, 50–52, 81; pregnancies resulting from gang rape, 21–22, 50–52; Quechua women's memory afflictions (toxic memories), 38–39, 49; strategic pregnancies, 43–45; studying how women talk about sexual violence, 46–48. *See also* environments and legacies of armed conflicts
Social Solidarity Network (Colombia), 63–64

sodomy and shame, 46
Solier, Magaly, 39
Standing Rock Sioux Reservation, 81
Stern, Maria, 19
stigma narratives and conflict-related sexual violence, 9–35, 93; and children's proper names (surnames), 20–22, 24, 99n34; disclosure issues, 23–26, 31–35; naming practices and children born of war, 13–22, 90; Peru and aftermath of internal armed conflict, 12–22; and Quechua women's memory afflictions (toxic memories), 38–39, 49; questions arising when stigma narrative is challenged, 11–12; and rejection of children born of war, 11–12; self-reinforcing dynamics and "looping effects" created by categories and classifications, 10; sodomy and shame, 46; and UK's *Principles for Global Action* policy document, 9–10
strategic pregnancies, 43–45; having the child of a *comunero*, 44–45; and narratives of women's heroism, 43–45; women exercising of control over reproductive labor, 44–45
"Surfacing Children" (Carpenter), 45
"survivor-centered" approaches and perspectives, 5
Survivor's Fund Rwanda (SURF), 23–25

TallBear, Kim, 40, 58
La teta asustada (The Milk of Sorrow) (film), 39
Tierra Digna (land rights organization), 77
Todd, Zoe, 58
Toledo, Alejandro, 18
Tomayro, Señora, 44–45, 50
transitional justice processes: accountability approaches, 21, 30, 89, 94, 98n24; Colombia's, 30–35, 75–82, 94; and reparations programs, 30–31, 88–89. *See also* Colombia's transitional justice process; reparations
trauma, historical or intergenerational, 39–40. *See also* epigenetics

Uganda, 16–17
UNICEF, 50
United Nations Basic Principles and Guidelines on the Right to a Remedy and Reparation for Victims of Gross Violations of International Human Rights Law and Serious Violations of International Humanitarian Law, 76
United Nations Convention on the Rights of the Child (Article 7.1), 20
United Nations Department of Peacekeeping Operations (DPKO), 33, 35
United Nations High Commissioner for Refugees, 63–66
United Nations Security Council Resolutions (UNSCR) of the Women, Peace and Security

Agenda, 4–5, 93; foundational Resolution 1325, 4–5; Resolution 2122 and access to health services resulting from rape, 4; Resolution 2467 and children born of conflict-related sexual violence, 5; Resolution 2467 and women and girls who become pregnant as a result of sexual violence, 4–5
United Nations Special Rapporteur on Violence Against Women, 3–4
United States Agency for International Development (USAID), 49–50
United States Foreign Assistance Act, 50
Unit for the Search for Persons Presumed Disappeared (Colombia), 77
Urabá region of Colombia, 7, 58–73; Afro-Colombian communities, 7, 59; Andalusia, 63–73; Apartadó, 61, 70, 75; Atrato River and river basin, 7, 59–73, 76–77; biodiversity, 59; Buena Vista, 65; campesinos and peace accords, 61–63; Costa de Oro, 63–73; Curvaradó, 64, 68–69; Domingodó, 64; FARC blockades on Atrato River, 65, 67–68, 72; the FARC in, 60–73; internally displaced persons, 60–61; international humanitarian commission accompanying villagers of Andalusia Peace Community to Costa de Oro, 63–73; local Catholic diocese, 61–62, 63–69; multiple ethnic and racial groups of, 7, 59; natural resource extraction, 60; paramilitaries in, 60–65, 69–73, 75–76; Peace Communities, 60, 61–73, 76–77; pollution and environmental degradation, 7, 59, 74; poverty and role of the war, 72–73; Riosucio (town), 64, 72, 73; the Río Sucio, 64–65; Turbo, 61, 64–65, 75; Villa Hermosa, 68–71; violence and struggles for control between paramilitaries and the FARC, 60–73, 75–77
Urban Walker, Margaret, 47–48
Uribe, Álvaro, 27–28, 29–30, 76

Van Ee, Elisa, 12, 14, 48, 105n9
"vernacular landscapes," 78
"Violence on the Land, Violence on Our Bodies" (Women's Earth Alliance and Native Youth Sexual Health Network), 53
Vom Bruck, Gabriele, 14–15, 99n34

war orphans, 7–8
"weapon of war" approach to rape, 19
Weitsman, Patricia, 23, 42–43
West, Robin, 90
Women, Peace and Security Agenda and UNSCR resolutions on conflict-related sexual violence, 4–5, 93
Wood, Elisabeth, 10–11, 47

Zraly, Maggie, 47